Living on the Land

Living on the Land

Change among the Inuit of Baffin Island

John S. Matthiasson

broadview press

Canadian Cataloguing in Publication Data

Matthiasson, John Stephen, 1936-
Living on the Land : Change among the Inuit of Baffin Island

ISBN 0-921149-93-X
1. Inuit - Northwest Territories - Baffin Island.
I. Title.
E&. M38 1992   971.9'503   C92-094869-3

© 1992, Broadview Press, Ltd.

Broadview Press
Post Office Box 1243, Peterborough, Ontario, Canada, K9J 7H5

in the United States of America
3576 California Road, Orchard Park, NY 14127

in the United Kingdom
c/o Drake Marketing, Saint Fagan's Road, Fairwater, Cardiff, CF53AE

Broadview Press gratefully acknowledges the support of the Canada Council,
the Ontario Arts Council, the Ontario Publishing Centre,
and the Ministry of National Heritage.

PRINTED IN CANADA
5 4 3 2   94 95 96

TABLE OF CONTENTS

ACKNOWLEDGEMENTS

The original field work which I carried out in Pond Inlet was supported by the Social Science Research Council of New York, New York. Support for the writing up of field notes was later provided by the National Institute of Mental Health, Washington, D.C. Ten years later, a grant from the Northern Studies Committee of the University of Manitoba allowed me to return to Pond Inlet. I am grateful for all three tangible expressions of assistance. Without them, there would have been no study, and anything I might have known about the of Baffin Island would have been gleaned from reading the books of other authors -- not personal experience.

I have a special debt I wish to recognize, and that is to Pertti J. Pelto, now of the University of Connecticut. Bert encouraged me to 'go north', when I had originally planned to head off for India for my doctoral research. While I was in the field, he left Cornell for the University of Minnesota, but kept in regular contact with me, telling me in letters to keep my spirits up, to have "dialogues with myself", in order to keep my anthropological perspective when my letters to him suggested that I was too involved in living as an Inuk and forgetting why I was there in the first place, and continued to treat me as 'his student.' I am deeply appreciative of his support, and acknowledge it here.

I also wish to pay homage to the help of Victor W. Turner, who left us so sadly and prematurely just a few years ago. Victor guided me in my dissertation writing, and thus to the first public expression of my experience of 'living on the land,' and whatever of anthropological value I had retrieved from it.

I have not used real names for the Kadluna of Pond Inlet of either period in the book. Perhaps they will not be offended if I express my collective thanks to them here. Bob Pilot, Rev. Howard Bracewell and Jim Haining assisted me during the first trip. Bill and Gwen Berry gave me opportunities to bathe and enjoy cuisine of my own culture when I accompanied the hunters into the settlement on trading expeditions, and encouraged me to write this book.

Most importantly, I acknowledge in humility the assistance of the Tununermiut, and in particular, the family of Reverend Jimmy Muckpah, who invited a young anthropologist and outsider into their lives, and shared them with him. At the time of my first field work, Elijah Erkloo and Paul Koolerk, both from Pond Inlet, were living in Ottawa. They assisted me in the translation of questionnaire data from Inuktitut to English, and I thank them for their diligence in that endeavor. Other Tununermiut, and especially the Aullativikmiut, are mentioned by name in the text, and I hope they realize my indebtedness to them.

Vera Gardner deserves a special note of thanks for her continued support during the last stages of writing and re-writing.

To everyone at Broadview Press who worked on the publication of the book, and Don Lepan, its president, in particular, a tip of the hat.

I dedicate this book to my children; Steve, a student of philosophy who helped his father understand Foucault and other writers, bicyclist, traveller and outdoors person, and Nancy, who among her other virtues, is a good mother to her girls and allows me grandfatherly indulgences of them.

Department of Anthropology

University of Manitoba

May 29, 1992

PREFACE

The Inuit of the Canadian Arctic, once known to outsiders as the Eskimo, created cultural forms that have fascinated readers since they were first described in print. School children from around the world know about the romantic people who lived in igloos and hunted sea mammals for food. Unfortunately, while accurate in part, this image of the Inuit, or "people," has often been romanticized and so has ignored a larger reality. Until recently, Inuit men and women laboured through a hard daily existence in what is perhaps the most demanding environment on the face of the earth. On their own, though, they and their ancestors have survived through several centuries, and created richly rewarding life-styles. Those life-styles went through a series of changes over time, as revealed in the archaeological record.

Change of a different type was imposed on the Inuit when their lands and the waters adjacent to them were discovered by Europeans. First came the explorers, in search of the fabled Northwest Passage, soon followed by the whalers, who interacted economically and socially with the Inuit they encountered but always returned with their catch to the ports from whence they came.

Later, outsiders came to Inuit country to stay. These were the missionaries, traders, and police. As the people worked at creating means to handle these intrusions, they suddenly found themselves part of a new nation-state — the nation of Canada. For some decades, Canadians showed little interest in the people who resided in the Arctic regions. This began to change when, for a variety of reasons, the Government of Canada initiated programs of directed change that encouraged the Inuit to move off the land. The implications of these programs were drastic — an almost total change in Inuit life-style.

Today, most Inuit live in settlements and hamlets, some of which have taken on urban attributes. If men hunt, they do so on weekends or during vacations. They work at wage labour, and the women cook on electric stoves and do the family washing in electric washing machines. Their children attend school and in their spare time listen to rock and western music on expensive stereo equipment or watch videos on VCRs. However, these contemporary Inuit, living what appears to be a southern life-style, are only a few decades away from life "on the land," and, more importantly, they have not given up their emotional ties with it.

I had a rare opportunity to participate in the life of a small population of Inuit living on northern Baffin Island in the high Arctic during a time when the rumblings of government-sponsored changes were still only murmurs. These are the Tununermiut, the majority of whom were still living on the land in small hunting camps, scattered around the settlement of Pond Inlet.

A decade later I returned to Pond Inlet to examine the changes the new federal programs had wrought and the responses of the Tununermiut to those changes. I was welcomed back by my friends, with whom I had maintained contact in the intervening years, and one invited me to stay in his new three-bedroom home.

I have in several scholarly articles attempted to describe those changes and the manner in which the people handled them. But it seemed that there was more to be said: a few years ago the daughter of Jimmy Muckpah, who is a central figure in this narrative, visited me in Winnipeg. Suzy is now a teacher in an Arctic community. I talked with her one evening about the camp life into which she had been born during the time I was living with her family, but of which she had only dim memories. The photographs I showed her of that life seemed to intrigue her, and she was soon showering me with a barrage of questions. Life on the land was as alien to her as it would be to the average southern teenager.

Suzy's visit prompted me to write a reflective and extended piece describing the Tununermiut camp life that disappeared shortly after I encountered it, and the impact of the intrusive federal government programs that led to its demise. This narrative is the result — I call it a personalized ethnography.

Even more personally, I have been moved to write this because I have an adopted daughter, Nancy, who is an Inuk by birth. Her world is partly defined by our family life, but for her there is the Inuit heritage as well. Nancy's daughters, Crystal and Cindy, know about the Inuit experience only through school books. For them, I want to provide an alternative representation.

Finally, my son, Steve, grew up with an older sister whose physical appearance differs from his. He should know something about her cultural past.

And so, I wrote this for my children and grandchildren, and for Suzy, who became a close friend of Nancy.

The story is as much about the anthropologist who came to live among the Tununermiut as it is about the people themselves, and so it includes an extended description of my entries into the setting. Still, I have tried to ensure that what follows is accurate. I hope that it will find a place in anthropology courses in the academy, but will also have an audience beyond that — one that includes the Inuit.

I have used the anthropological lenses that my discipline gives me to interpret events and processes — and what for me were the remarkable ways in which the people have coped with them. I have included a lengthy depiction of life in the camps before the move to the settlement, the way of life that was disrupted by the implementation of the federal policy. I also trace some of the influences of the whalers, because the waters surrounding northern Baffin Island were worked intensely by whalers, and the whaling period in Canadian Arctic history has often been neglected.

However, the focus is on the responses of the Tununermiut to imposed change, which responses were, in my opinion, truly remarkable. I acknowledge here, in, I hope, true humility, my profound debt to my friends and teachers — the Tununermiut of Pond Inlet; and I look forward to hearing whether the story recounted here rings true for them.

BECOMING LIKE AN INUIT?

Late in the summer of 1963 I stepped from an aircraft that had landed on the airstrip in Resolute Bay, Northwest Territories, a combined Royal Canadian Forces and Department of Transport base located on Cornwallis Island in the Canadian high Arctic. It was raining heavily; the wool suit I wore was soaked through before I set foot into the shack in which I was to stay for the next few days, waiting for an available aircraft to take me on the next leg of my journey to Pond Inlet, a small settlement on northern Baffin Island. My bunkmates in the shack were pilots, aircraft maintenance men, and a radio dispatcher, all associated with an oil exploration company based in a southern Canadian city. At the time I was a doctoral student in anthropology at Cornell University on my way to Pond Inlet to collect information on aspects of the life of the Tununermiut Inuit to be used as the basis for my dissertation. After securing transportation to the settlement, I was to remain there for the next thirteen months. Stated briefly, my main task was to describe traditional patterns of social control, and the influence on them of a Royal Canadian Mounted Police detachment in Pond Inlet. During my stay in the area I did make some observations relating to these concerns, but I also did one other thing that, in retrospect, may be of more importance: I participated in a way of life for which the death knell had already been tolled.

Ten years later, in the summer of 1973, I once again stepped from an aircraft in Resolute Bay. Instead of a shack, I found quarters in the fairly recently constructed Airhotel. Once again I waited for an available aircraft to take me to Pond Inlet, this time on a return trip of combined nostalgia and anthropological comparison. I was soon to become aware of the numerous changes that had occurred in the high Arctic in the intervening decade.

When I first arrived in Pond Inlet, on the northeastern tip of Baffin Island, I had planned to spend a year working with Inuit informants and observing day-to-day Inuit life. Before leaving for the "field" I had been led to believe that there were several bilingual Inuit in the area, and that it would be an easy matter to hire one or more as interpreters. I was uncertain of where I would find accommodation, but certain that something would show up. No one in the settlement knew of my impending arrival, although I was equipped with an Explorer's and Scientist's license properly signed by the appropriate officials in Ottawa — a bureaucratic prerequisite for research in the Northwest Territories. In the early 1960s flights to and from isolated settlements such as Pond Inlet were infrequent and irregular. The bush pilot who brought me from Resolute Bay to Pond Inlet had never made the trip before, but he had a good set of maps and strong faith in his ability to follow them. The commanding officer of the Resolute RCAF base came along for the ride, having provided me, a graduate student on a limited budget, with free meals at the base during my stay in Resolute. We approached Pond Inlet from behind the high hill that forms a long ridge behind it, and landed on a relatively smooth strip of land. After climbing from the aircraft and dumping my luggage on the ground, we walked over the hill and down into the settlement proper where we identified the RCMP post and knocked on the door of the attached residence. The corporal who answered us was startled but quickly recovered his composure, invited us into his home, and offered all a cup of tea. No one in the settlement had heard the approaching aircraft or seen it land.

Before the aircraft departed again, the corporal asked to see my license and inspected it carefully, particularly in light of my stated research concern with legal change and the influence of the RCMP presence on the local Inuit. Finding the license in order, he immediately began to look for accommodation for me, and eventually arranged a temporary stay in a vacant teacherage until something more permanent could be located. (Teachers in northern communities commonly "go south" in summers to attend university summer school programs.) It was with a feeling of great satisfaction that I unrolled my sleeping bag that evening, made a pot of coffee, and reflected on the fact that I had arrived — I was finally "in the field."

As I mentioned earlier, my purpose in making the trek to Pond Inlet was to observe and describe factors related to what I called legal acculturation, or the transition from traditional Inuit forms of social control to a reliance on Canadian law enforcement officers and an observance of federal and territorial laws. I now realize that I had been extremely naïve. For example, I had thought that I could carry out my field operations while comfortably ensconced in the settlement. I had neglected to find out before my departure that most of the Inuit of the Pond Inlet area lived, not in the settlement, but in small camps located from eight to one hundred and fifty miles from it. In most cases they were full-time hunters and living, as northerners say, "on the land." It soon became apparent to me that if I lived in the settlement I would not have much opportunity to record the types of information in which I was interested. It also became quickly apparent that if I was to do my interviewing I would have to learn the Inuit language, Inuktitut, for, despite what I had been told in the south, there were no fully bilingual Inuit in the area. Many of the Euro-Canadians in the settlement were fluent in the Inuit language, but they had their own jobs to do and had no time to act as interpreters for an itinerant graduate student in anthropology.

During my first days in Pond Inlet I did what most anthropologists do who realize that the language problem is going to be stickier than anticipated. I walked about the settlement (or, more accurately, since it consisted in the main of a long line of buildings strung out along the coast, walked back and forth), trying to form impressions and decide how in the world I was going to begin my research. Everyone in the settlement seemed to have something to do except me, but I did gain impressions, draw maps, and read a great many mystery novels that I had borrowed from the Hudson's Bay Company trader.

In the summer of 1963 Pond Inlet was on the threshold of a series of transitions that were to alter it permanently, and that would act as catalysts for other modifications of the community and the people, modifications that have continued into the 1990s. But these changes had not yet occurred, and I was able to view a Canadian Arctic settlement that was in many ways typical during the late 1950s and early 1960s. Many observers have claimed for Pond Inlet the distinction of being the most attractively situated settlement in northern Canada. I have only heard this claim disputed by those with an attachment to Pangnirtung, but since I have not visited Pangnirtung myself I cast my vote with those who glorify Pond Inlet, for it is indeed beautifully situated. Twenty miles across Eclipse Sound are the frozen glacial rivers and majestic snow-capped mountains of Bylot Island, rising as high as six thousand feet out of the water and looking from a distance like a long multi-coloured comb standing on its back. A short walk over the hills that create a backdrop for the settlement finds one surrounded by mountain landscapes on all sides, with rolling vistas of tundra in the immediate range of vision.

Situated at latitude 72° 44' and longitude 78° 00', Pond Inlet is one of the most northern Inuit settlements in Canada, and in-

Summer camp of Aullativikmiut, 1963

deed, one of the most northern sites of human habitation in the world. Traditionally rich in fish and seal, the waters that it faces have long provided an economic base for the Inuit people themselves, and more recently for the traders who created the basis for a stable, permanent settlement. In 1963 the first impression the visitor to Pond Inlet received was of a row of buildings housing the various agencies with established contingents in the community. These were the RCMP, which maintained a two-man detachment (with only the one corporal resident at the time), the Hudson's Bay Company (HBC) trading post, Anglican and Roman Catholic missions, and a fledgling Department of Northern Affairs (DNA) contingent comprising an area administrator, a mechanic, and two school teachers, along with their families. Each grouping had its own cluster of buildings, and the DNA, which had only recently entered the community but was rapidly taking over its administration, had been forced to break new ground at the extreme northern edge near the glacial creek that provided the community water supply in summer months. Their buildings were still surrounded by mud and broken tundra, unlike the grass-covered grounds of the older and more established agencies.

A few Inuit lived in the settlement — mainly aged widows and families employed by Euro-Canadian agencies[1] — but most lived on the land and visited the settlement every month or so to trade seal skins and fox furs for such items as flour, tea, sugar, and cloth. There were several outlying camps in 1963, which I will describe in greater detail in a later chapter. As I acquainted myself with the settlement during my first few days there, I realized that I would have to arrange to live for at least a few months in one or more of these camps if I was to achieve any of my research aims. Along with other factors such as the language barrier, there was one further problem with staying in the settlement: a sharp social gap existed between Euro-Canadians and the Inuit. There was very little interaction between the two, and by remaining there I would inadvertently but also unavoidably identify myself with the Euro-Canadian side; my contacts with the Inuit would be sharply circumscribed, if not non-existent. So, before I had been in Pond Inlet for a week, I began to explore ways to establish myself in a camp.

Of course, not knowing a word of the Inuit language, Inuktitut, I had no means of communicating with "land people" when they were in the settlement other than to exchange a smile when I came across them. Once again RCMP corporal Robert Pilot came to my assistance. I explained my predicament to him and he agreed to try and find a camp family that would be willing to take me in as a boarder. All land people visited the RCMP quarters when in the settlement, and after about a week Corporal Pilot called me into his office to tell me that Jimmy Muckpah, a young man from a camp mid-distance from Pond Inlet, was prepared to consider having me move in with him and his family. A meeting was arranged between the two of us, in which Bob Pilot acted as interpreter, and it was decided that I would accompany Bob on his patrol of the camps the following week and be dropped off at Aullativik, the camp that was to become my home for the next nine months.

I had borrowed an Inuit parka from the Department of Northern Affairs stores in Ottawa, but it didn't fit — I am over six feet tall — and during my brief stay in Resolute Bay I had been informed, with great glee, that it was actually a woman's parka. In any event I soon realized that it was insufficient to keep my thin southern blood warm, and the boots I had purchased before leaving the south were less than adequate for extended periods out of doors unless I kept my feet in perpetual motion. Consequently, I was miserable during the trip to Aullativik and spent most of the time huddled in an open space behind the small cabin trying to keep warm. The other men were standing outside, and I felt I should do the same. We visited several other camps on the way and arrived at the summer camp of the Aullativikmiut late in the

Preparations for a day of hunting.

afternoon of our second day out. I had dinner with Bob in his tent and then, having decided, on Bob's advice, to make the break with the outside world as quickly as possible, spent the night in the tent of Jimmy Muckpah. That first evening and the day that followed were not easy for me, nor for my Inuit hosts — I will describe them in some detail later — but for better or worse, I was to be a guest of Jimmy and his family for most of the next nine months.

Although he and I were the same age, Jimmy would refer to me as his son, and indeed he took seriously the task of training me in Inuit male skills, as he would do with his real son when he was old enough. I had not been sure how best to characterize my reasons for wanting to live in a camp, and not having any command of the Inuit language, I had asked Corporal Pilot to explain to Jimmy that I simply wanted to learn to be like an Inuit and to live like them. It seemed too difficult to explain my interest in legal acculturation. Today I would be more honest about my research goals, regardless of linguistic or conceptual difficulties, but as events developed during my stay with the Aullativikmiut, the reasons given at the time turned out to be not far from the truth. Before long I found myself becoming increasingly neglectful of my research aims and collection of the data that would enable me to accomplish them, and instead spending most of my time attempting

Atagootung, matriarch of Aullativik.

to master the skills to which I was being daily exposed. Two weeks after my arrival, when the people moved back to their winter camp at Aullativik on Curry Island, desire to learn to behave as an Inuit adult male was intensified. While the men made the trip in their motor-driven canoes and other small craft, I was forced to travel with the women and children in the large bulky whale-boat, a cruel blow to my male ego.

Before many weeks had passed I began to feel a part of camp life and the camp community. There were five households, and soon I was visiting freely in all of them. A few of the younger children had at first been frightened by me, but before long they seemed to accept me. I am mistrustful of anthropological colleagues who speak of being "adopted" by the people with whom they work, and I was certainly not adopted by Jimmy and his family, for my physical size, colouring, and linguistic background marked me as ineradicably different. But I was accepted, or at least tolerated, and before long I felt a part of my surroundings. In time I lost the status of stranger and alien.

The period of initial adjustment was greatly facilitated by the kindness and hospitality that Jimmy, his family, and the other Aullativikmiut extended to me, but it was by no means easy. The meal I ate in Bob's tent my first evening in the camp was to be my last "southern" meal for some time to come. After the long and cold boat trip we relished the hearty stew made from canned vegetables and frozen beef; as we sat about afterwards sipping on mugs of coffee, Bob suggested that I spend my first night with Jimmy's family in their tent. I agreed; while he made the necessary arrangements, I looked at Jimmy's small canvas tent and experienced my first real feelings of trepidation. Hanging from the guide-ropes were strips of raw fish, which I assumed might be the meal for the next day (it turned out that I was correct). Later in the evening I brought my sleeping bags over to the tent and laid them down, one inside of the other, at the edge of the cloth that had been spread out on the frozen ground. I did not sleep well that night; I was very conscious of being an intruder in someone else's bed, as we slept side by side with the two adult Inuit on one side, the two children in the middle, and myself at the other side.

The following morning I shared some bannock and tea with the family, then went over to watch Bob pack up his gear for the trip to the next camp on his itinerary. I then stood alone on the shore and pensively observed them pull away. A few yards out, Bob turned back to me and called, "See you in a couple of months. Take care of yourself!" I didn't miss the note of humour in his voice, and as I stood there I realized that "a couple of months" was *accurate*. The Aullativikmiut had only recently been in to the settlement to trade, and would not be returning for at least another six weeks, perhaps longer. Bob's last call to me was to be the last English I would hear, other than my own voice, for some time to come. I have to admit that a wave of apprehension and even of fear swept over me; I have never felt so isolated and alone before or since. Now I was truly in the field.

Before leaving the settlement I had purchased materials for a parka, and during the next several days Jimmy's wife, Elisapee, worked diligently at making one for me. It took her some time, because she had never made one so large, and she had to pull it apart and begin over again more than once. I was taller than the other men by several inches, but was also considerably overweight at the time. During the next few months I would lose forty pounds from running beside dogsleds and existing on a diet almost entirely of meat, but initially the parka had to be wide enough to gird my excessive girth. I was grateful when the parka was completed and she had time to begin making me a pair of sealskin boots and dufflecloth socks. She had the same problem of size with the boots. One of the other women agreed to knit a multicoloured Inuit cap for me, with a long tassel that would hang outside the parka hood in front, keeping the fur trim close to my face. It kept the head from falling forward. When all of my new clothing was completed, it, along with a cast-off pair of overpants that Bob Pilot had given me, allowed me to walk about the camp in some comfort.

Earlier I wrote that Bob's stew was to be my last southern meal for a while. I might not have waited so long, since I had purchased food supplies in the settlement. But I gave my cache to Jimmy so that his family might share them with me, and on my first day in the camp he gave them all away to the other families. This was my first example of traditional Inuit sharing practices, and its expression on that occasion meant that I was to learn to eat land food more quickly than I had anticipated. At first I was only given bannock and pieces of heart and liver from seals, sometimes raw and other times cooked, and occasionally fish. The people were aware that southerners very often refuse to eat seal meat, and if they do accept it, restrict themselves to liver or heart, neither of which has quite the strong taste of other cuts. I soon tired of the organ cuts, so some of the first words I learned in the Inuktitut language were those for other cuts of meat.

Throughout my stay with the Aullativikmiut I was a source of concern to my hosts — although less so as I toughened up physically and learned traditional skills — but they were particularly worried about me during my second week in camp. Possibly because of the diet, or the stress of adapting to the cold, I became seriously ill. Unable to eat, I lay in my sleeping bag for days, only rousing myself for an occasional mug of hot tea. All of the Inuit were extremely solicitous, and I think that Jimmy was especially worried about how he would explain my death to the RCMP. In time my strength and appetite returned, with the illness having forged a new bond between me and Jimmy. The following week a young child became ill, running a high fever and causing distress to his parents. Once again, the camp members collectively showed their concern for the discomfort of an individual. It was suggested, more by gesture than by words, that I might be able to help him, but there was nothing I felt I could do, although I desperately wished that I could. The first night all of the women crowded together in the boy's family's tent, maintaining a vigil with the mother, while the men stayed awake playing cards in another tent. By morning the fever had broken, and soon the child was up and about playing with his friends.

Some casual observers have claimed that the Inuit are a people devoid of normal emotions, who do not express grief at their own or others' misfortunes. I was quickly disabused of this stereotype by the preceding two examples of anxiety and concern over individual suffering. In time I learned to view the Inuit as a stoic people — the exigencies of their environment had made them so — but these two examples among others demonstrated to me their depths of feeling for others. There was no gnashing of teeth or open display of emotion, but the concern was always apparent, in other, more subtle ways.

Over time, of course, the basic problems I encountered on entering the field were largely overcome, and I became something of a fixture in the camp. I became immersed, as much as possible, in its daily life, but not before I had passed through all of the stages of culture shock, with the fluctuating emotions characteristic of it. There were times when I was almost overwhelmed by paranoia, feeling that I was an object of ridicule for everyone from the headman to the smallest child. At those times the very utterance of the word *Kadluna*, which is the all-embracing term for everyone who is not an Inuk, would plunge me into despair, for I would be convinced that I was being laughed at or disparaged. There were also moments when I felt a great sense of contentment and peace, such as in the early mornings when the other members of the household and I would lie under our sleeping robes (or, in my case, my sleeping bag), drinking tea brewed over a primus stove and munching on bannock.

My moments of paranoia may have had some basis in fact, for I know that my presence stretched to the limits the tolerance of the Aullativikmiut, but they were always gentle hosts, and they and I somehow accommodated ourselves to one another and weathered the next nine months. There were many skills I had to master before I could truly be said to have participated in Inuit male life, and some of them I never did become proficient in. After some months had passed, the men began to refer to me as *Inoongwa*, which meant, they told me, that I had become a person who was "in the image of an Inuk." I doubt that I have ever been as flattered by anything in my life, except for the time, not long after, when they told me that I was now an Inuk myself. (I never was, of course, and never could be, but I was immensely delighted.) The latter occurred when Jimmy and I were visiting a nearby camp while on a hunting trip, and our hostess began to wash a mug for me as we prepared to have tea. Jimmy told her not to bother, and later explained to me that he had done so because I was an Inuk, and so the niceties of Kadluna behaviour were not necessary. The day that Jimmy first asked me to take his dog team and go out on the ice to see about the status of his seal nets, I felt like an Inuk, as

I did on the first evening when, after a long day of travelling, the men went into the newly built snowhouse to drink tea and left me outside to feed the dogs. I knew that they no longer were worried about my survival in their world.

I find it difficult to write about the Tununermiut and their way of life in a detached, objective manner, for as much as possible, that way of life became my own for the better part of a year. I tried to do so in articles I have published in anthropological journals, but I have always felt a sense of unreality in the attempt. I became a different person during those nine months. It has been said that the first major field trip for an anthropologist is similar to the experience of going through depth psychoanalysis. This was true of me, for my visions of my own personhood and the social worlds in which I exist were changed irreversibly. One leaves the field with an altered perspective on the human condition and, often, a permanently modified personality. We anthropologists are even as affected by our field work as are our informants and those who read our writings, and perhaps even more so.

I also believe very strongly that the writings of the anthropologist can never be divorced from the anthropologist him- or herself. The thoughts and feelings of anthropologists are the filters through which their observations are transformed into data, and so for me, the "anthropologist as variable" is perhaps the most critical part of the equation that begins on entry into the field and culminates in journal articles, a monograph, or whatever type of publication. The personal responses of the anthropologist deserve to be more than anecdotes recounted year after year to classes of undergraduates. I have always felt a sense of artificiality in my more "professional" writings on the Inuit, in which I have attempted to keep myself out of the picture. I will not attempt to do so here, and if this lacks the seeming rigour of a purely professional piece of writing, it will hopefully have more humanity to it. The material of the following chapters presents the perceptions of John Matthiasson at two different periods of his life, and it is influenced by all of his prejudices, preferences and values, and inadequacies. I hope that it also has some anthropological value.

After spending nine months with the Aullativikmiut, I returned to Pond Inlet for several months, with intermittent periods being spent in other camps and three weeks in late spring back in Aullativik. Thirteen months after my arrival with the bush pilot and the RCAF officer, I left for the south.

In the summer of 1973, ten years later, I returned to Pond Inlet. The camps were no more; Aullativik was nothing but a cluster of decaying houses. All of the Tununermiut Inuit had moved from the camps into the settlement. On this visit I was not concerned specifically with legal change; I wanted to document some of the events that had occurred during the intervening decade. Jimmy Muckpah had become an ordained Anglican minister, with a mission post of his own in Eskimo Point on the west coast of Hudson Bay. Many of the young men worked on oil rigs. In a profound sense, a way of life had disappeared, and the old men who had been camp bosses told me that they grieved at its passing. In the following chapters I attempt, from my own perspective, to document some of the changes that took place, the historical factors that preceded them, and some of their consequences for the Tununermiut, my friends and teachers.

Note

1   It has become fairly standard practice in writings on the Canadian Inuit to refer to non-Inuit by the term which the Inuit themselves use for such people: *kabloona, kabluna, kapluna, kadluna,* or some other variation, depending on which orthography one uses (Vallee, 1962). I prefer to employ the term coined by John Honigmann, "Euro-Canadian" (Honigmann & Honigmann, 1965), which is a more accurate description of contact agents in Arctic Canada, at least during the 1960s. That is, in the contact-traditional period the major exemplars of non-Inuit behaviour, values, and institutions to the Inuit were not Canadians but HBC employees recruited in Scotland, Anglican missionaries from England, and Roman Catholic priests from Belgium and France. More recently, large numbers of European immigrants have found employment in Arctic settlements as teachers, mechanics, and bureaucrats. We should also remember that it was Scottish whalers, not Canadians or Americans, who introduced the whaling industry and all of its acculturative effects to the Pond Inlet area. I think these facts are important in understanding the socio-psychological dynamics of Tununermiut acculturation. The European influence has always been as potent as the Canadian, although this situation is changing today. For these reasons, then, I will use "Euro-Canadian" throughout the remainder of the text.

A WHALING WE WILL GO

I will later describe in some detail the life-style of the Tununer-miut who lived in camps, and specifically the daily routines of the people of Aullativik. We shall encounter the Euro-Canadians who lived in Pond Inlet during the early 1960s, and will examine the effects of their presence on Tununermiut life. Helm and Damas (1963), in an influential article, have characterized Inuit camp life of that period as "contact-traditional." The term is appropriate, for although many features of traditional Inuit society and culture were still evident in camps, the Inuit residents were irrevocably en-meshed with Euro-Canadian institutions.

Three main tentacles of Euro-Canadian society had reached into the Arctic and created the contact-traditional period for the Tununermiut and other Inuit across Arctic Canada. These were the Hudson Bay Company, the Royal Canadian Mounted Police, and Christian missionary movements. The Inuit had indeed become de-pendent on all three; but they had also preserved a separate cul-tural identity and existence, and to a considerable extent they had been encouraged to do so by the southerners. The HBC wanted fox pelts and seal skins, and only by hunting could the Inuit provide them. The RCMP did not want to see the Inuit become dependent on welfare, or to have a rising crime rate (in terms of Canadian definitions of crime), and so encouraged them to live away from the settlements. Roman Catholic and Anglican missionaries feared secularization and moral corruption stemming from settlement life, with its attendant greater contact with outsiders. It was in the in-terest of all three agencies, therefore, to keep the people living out "on the land" in the camps. Nevertheless, during the contact-tradi-tional period the Tununermiut did not live fully as their ancestors had done. Instead, they traded their furs for foodstuffs, cloth, can-vas, tobacco, and other sundries. They observed, insofar as they understood them, federal and territorial laws, and in particular, the game ordinances. Finally, although they continued to practise both shamanism and animism, which I discuss in a later chapter, they had become devout Christians.

When I first visited the Tununermiut, the contact-traditional period was in its last stage, and soon the people were to enter what I have elsewhere termed the "period of centralization." There would be a mass migration from the camps to the settlement. The people would come under the influence of planned change directed by government policies and carried out by federal and territorial civil servants. The consequences of that change, or what I call "intervention acculturation" were not precisely what the planners anticipated, but they were profound and irreversible. Few human populations have ever experienced such dramatic social and cultural disruption in one generation as did the Tununermiut Inuit in the 1960s and 1970s. What happened to them was similar to transformations experienced by Inuit across the Canadian Arctic, as they all entered the period of centralization. But these were not the first effects the Tununermiut were to encounter as a result of contact with outsiders.

Although my primary concern here is with the transition from the contact-traditional to the centralization periods, it is important to briefly examine some of the cultural history of the Tununermiut themselves, and the acculturation processes that influenced them as they moved from a traditional way of life to contact-traditional.

Pre-Contact Period

The Inuit of the Canadian Arctic were nomadic people who travelled across the tundra in search of food. In most regions they did not begin to centre their movements on specific areas until the establishment of trading posts, on which they quickly became economically dependent for trade goods. Most Inuit, then, shifted the nucleus of their hunting activities to the environs of the nearest trading post, and the post was usually established at a coastal location easily accessible to supply ships. The Tununermiut, however, had lived in and around what was to become the settlement of Pond Inlet long before any Europeans or Euro-Canadians began using the same area for their own exploitative purposes. It had been their traditional hunting and residential area, over which they had roamed freely, as had populations before them. According to the dean of Arctic anthropology, Diamond Jenness, "A thousand years have passed since Pond Inlet welcomed its first inhabitants, or at least the first of whom we have any record" (Jenness, 1936: 14).

In early pre-contact times, when the Arctic lands that were to become Canada were the exclusive territory of the Inuit, small bands had lived and roamed on the islands north of Baffin Island, at the northeast tip of which Pond Inlet is located, but by the time the European ships began working these waters, the Tununermiut were probably the most northerly peoples of the North American Arctic (Jenness, 1936: 20). There is evidence that some of the earliest Inuit colonists to the Pond Inlet region lived at least briefly on the sandy shore of Button Point on Bylot Island, twenty or so miles across Eclipse Sound from the site of the present settlement. Jenness claimed that the inhabitants of Button Point wandered in search of game as far north as the eastern shores of Smith Sound, and even to Lake Hazen, some five hundred miles from the North Pole. There is no conclusive evidence as to the eventual fate of these people, but archaeological reconstruction shows that they were before long replaced by a new population of colonists from the west. The original inhabitants may have moved on, or been absorbed or even annihilated by their successors.

Some participants in this second wave continued past Baffin Island and the site of what is now Pond Inlet through the northern islands to Greenland. They were later joined by waves of migrants who had probably sojourned on northern Baffin. Those who first arrived in Greenland travelled south along the western shore of that massive ice-capped island, and in time they encountered the Norse settlements that had been founded in southern Greenland by Eric the Red and his followers after his exile from Iceland (Jenness, 1936: 20).

A third period of Inuit possession of the Pond Inlet region occurred in the fourteenth century, and once again, some representatives made their way onward to Greenland, settling along the northwestern coast. Others remained behind. These became the ancestors of the present-day Tununermiut; it was their descendants who met the first European exploration parties and whaling crews to arrive in the area. The connections between Tununermiut and Greenlanders was to be formed again, but not until the twentieth century.

Pond Inlet and its environs, then, had experienced a long history of human habitation before the first contact with outsiders, or non-Inuit peoples. This contact would in time usher in the contact-traditional period and ultimately the period of centralization, which rang the death knell for that way of life.

Missionaries, police, and traders created the foundation for the contact-traditional period for the Tununermiut, but by the time the former arrived on northern Baffin Island the Inuit had already had considerable experience with non-Inuit outsiders. The contact came not via southern Canadians, although they had some contact with these during the nineteenth century, but rather with whalers from the British Isles. The waters surrounding Pond Inlet were rich in whale life, and the area became a wintering spot for whaling crews. I believe that there is a cultural pattern of response to new experience that Inuit employ, and that it was used in their contact with the whalers. The pattern is essentially one of "watch and wait." It seems to me that Inuit will not commit themselves quickly or in a facile manner. They look at a new situation, and then withdraw to consider it and all of its implications. On the next encounter, they will have gained experience from the first, and will use this. What I am suggesting is that the way in which the Tununermiut responded to missionaries, police, traders, and, later, government officials and civil servants may have been largely determined by their earlier exposure to whalers, and so those earlier experiences are worthy of at least brief attention.

By the time the whaling industry reached its peak, the Tununermiut had become citizens of Canada. This occurred through a series of parliamentary elections that had an administrative effect on the Inuit of the Canadian Arctic, but little real impact. On June 22, 1869, the Canadian Parliament passed an act providing for temporary government of what had been known as Rupert's Land and the North-western Territory by the government of the new nation. As a consequence, all Inuit became, at least nominally, citizens of Canada. However, not until the following year, on June 23, 1870, did the Parliament of Great Britain pass the Rupert's Land Act, placing Rupert's Land and the North-western Territory under the permanent jurisdiction of Canada, and so fully admitting them into the three-year old union (Flanagan, 1963: 3).

Until that time the region, which would now be known as the Northwest Territories, had been a possession of the Hudson's Bay Company. In 1880, the remaining British lands in the Arctic archipelago were added to them (Lesage, 1955: 5). In fact, however, the transfer was in essence nothing more than a formality for the Inuit peoples who lived within the territories, and would remain such for the remainder of the nineteenth century. Two federal government expeditions were sent north in 1885-1886 and 1897 to study

Hunters breaking camp.

navigation conditions in Hudson Strait, but they seem to have had little if any influence on the Inuit who encountered them. Certainly the administrative and jurisdictional changes of the nineteenth century had no significant impact on the Tununermiut, who were busy creating economic and other relationships with whalers from Scotland.

During the latter half of the nineteenth century the whaling industry became a major economic enterprise in Europe and the United States, although perhaps less so in Canada. Different parts of the massive sea mammal's carcass were used to meet a variety of consumer demands, such as the bone for the manufacture of stays for women's corsets and gowns. The value of whales is suggested in a statement by Captain A.P. Low of the D.G.S. *Neptune*, which anchored near what was to become the settlement of Pond Inlet in 1903:

> Several species of whale are found in the waters of the northern ice-laden seas, but there is only one prize, known amongst other names as the Greenland whale, Right whale and Bowhead whale, and scientifically called *Balaena Mysticetus*. From its mouth is obtained the precious whale-bone. An average whale carries nearly a ton of this material, which at present is worth

about $15,000 a ton, with the price rising from year to year. The principal users of the whale-bone are to stiffen the bodices of the better-made gowns, and to weave into expensive silk fabrics. The wealth of the world is increasing and the supply of whales is decreasing; no idea, therefore, can be formed of the value of whale-bone in the future, as no good substitute has been discovered. An adult female will furnish blubber sufficient for nearly thirty tons of oil, while a male will supply about twenty tons. The value of oil is also on the increase, and may be taken at about $100 per ton. Thus, the total value of a large whale varies from $15,000 to $20,000. (Low, 1906: 249)

It is small wonder that men could be found in the Scottish and American ports who were willing to spend months or even a year at a time living on small ships in the Arctic waters in pursuit of whales, and others were prepared to finance such trips. For the first time, a non-renewable Arctic resource was being exploited, as Captain Low anticipated, almost to the point of extinction.

The whalers had a considerable amount of influence on the Inuit whom they encountered on their expeditions. This influence was primarily economic in nature but extended beyond the economic sphere. South of the Tununermiut, in Hudson Strait, there was intensive contact between both Scottish and American whalers and local Inuit, with the Inuit often being employed by the crews. It was not uncommon for several Inuit families to be taken onboard an American ship in early summer, for example, and to remain aboard until the ship left for home in October. The Inuit employees hunted both whale and walrus, skinned carcasses, and prepared walrus hides. They were paid in trade goods such as iron implements, tobacco, and cloth, on which items they soon became dependent. Farther north the waters were exploited more actively by the Scottish than the American crews, however, and since Scottish captains tended to rely almost exclusively on their own crews to perform virtually all duties, native economic dependency on outsiders was not as intense. It was Scottish ships that worked the water near Pond Inlet and the Tununermiut.

Nevertheless, the interaction between the Baffin Bay whalers and the Inuit they encountered, including the Tununermiut, was quite intensive and undoubtably had a lasting impact on the latter. The captains of many ships made what, in retrospect, were remarkably accurate and objective descriptions of Inuit culture and social arrangements, recording their observations in personal diaries and ship logs. The Canadian Inuit have a longstanding reputation as being keen observers, and although they had no means to record their observations on paper, it is most likely that they made correspondingly penetrating observations of the whalers. Personally, I await the day when the Inuit begin to do their own ethnography, for they seem to have a cultural flair for it. Not only are they typically good at observation, but they also tend to be reflective and analytic about their observations. These talents may be products of long experience as hunters, and a couple of centuries of contact with puzzling and often frustrating outsiders. I also believe that these observational skills are an important part of the explanation of Inuit representational art, in both carvings and silk-screen productions. In other words, I am suggesting that these talents might be lost within a new generation that has not been socialized to a hunting way of life, and that takes the presence of outsiders for granted. In any event, I believe that early contact with whalers, and Inuit perceptions of them and their behaviour, was important in the formation of later responses to outsiders.

The earliest recorded contact between northern Baffin Island Inuit and outsiders occurred in 1823, when Admiral William E. Parry cast anchor near what is now the settlement of Igloolik, several hundred miles south of Pond Inlet (Parry later visited the Pond Inlet area). At the time of this pre-whaler encounter, gifts of iron and needles were presented to the Iglulingmiut, along with other items. One aged woman from Pond Inlet, who had been visiting in the area, later recalled the event with typical Inuit humour and pragmatism. "When the white man's boat arrived at Iglulik, the Eskimos received biscuits and tobacco; how they would make the biscuits skip on the water and make them roll on the ground. As for the tobacco, they did not like its odor ... so they simply threw it away" (Mary-Rousselliere, 1957: 14). If the biscuits were pilot biscuits, which they probably were, the Inuit found a better use for them than trying to eat the incredibly leaden concoctions. It is unfortunate that the initial aversion to tobacco did not become a part of their cultural inventory, for in later years Inuit across Arctic Canada were to suffer from virtual epidemics of tuberculosis and, in time, lung cancer, surely linked to heavy smoking.

It was not until the early 1860s that the whaling crews began to work the very northern waters and that contact was of longer duration, but my point is that by the time the whalers arrived, the Tununermiut had already had some experience with the outside world and its alien ways. They had had time to reflect on it and the people who brought knowledge of it, and on ways in which they would relate to any newcomers who might follow Parry and other early explorers. We shall never know, of course, how these earlier encounters influenced later ones, and so we can only speculate, but they were important.

What we do know is that when the whaling industry moved into the northern waters surrounding Baffin Island, it did so with a figurative vengeance, and cast an indelible mark on the people of the region. Even if the Scottish whaling captains tended to use their own crews more than did their American counterparts, they did hire local Inuit for different tasks, traded with them, and gave crews shore leave to mix with them.

The whaling industry peaked at about the turn of the century. In 1903, at its zenith, Captain James A. Mutch of the whaler *Albert*, from Dundee, Scotland, could record in his log that he had encountered four other ships between Pond Inlet and Clyde River, a fairly short stretch along the north-eastern coast of Baffin Island, and had received word of another that had been lost near Melville Bay (Mutch, 1906: 487). By that time, it will be recalled, the Inuit had been titular citizens of Canada for several decades, but were far more influenced by Scottish whalers than by the new Canada. Canadian law was not enforced in the high Arctic, and Inuit continued to live outside of it and according to a customary Inuit code. An example of the effect of the change in legal status is revealed in part in another of Captain March's log entries.

> When close to Qivitung at Cape Hooper, a few Eskimos came off ... besides these, with their wives and families, a few were close to Padli. I asked those in the boat to come with me to Ponds Bay; but they were afraid of the Ponds Bay Eskimos, as there were so many murders up there. (Mutch, 1906: 485)

Jimmy Muckpah once told me the story of those same murders. We were passing an outcrop near our camp one day when he pointed to it and said that a "very bad man" had lived there many years before, and had begun to kill all of the people who lived with him. According to Jimmy, the survivors picked up their belongings and moved to Igloolik for a period of time. We do not have accurate statistics, but what evidence we have from early Arctic ethnographic accounts, as well as those of even earlier observers as Mutch, suggests that homicide was fairly common among the Inuit. It was often provoked by competition over women, but in the case Jimmy recounted to me the murderer was surely insane. In any event, by 1903 Canadian law had not reached up to the high Arctic.

During the whaling period, however, the Tununermiut were being influenced by other institutions of the alien societies that had sent intruders into their territories, even if their new legal and political status meant little to them. There is evidence, for example, that they were quick to come to grips with the capitalistic ethic practised by the whalers with whom they had contact. Much to the consternation of the whalers, as the following quotation illustrates, the Inuit became shrewd bargainers who were unwilling to be economically exploited. Perhaps there was an aboriginal economic base for their dealings with outsiders, but that is difficult to determine.

> The real Ponds Bay Eskimo had been coming and going all winter, trading a fox-skin when they had one, but always wanting nearly the home value for it or for anything they might bring. They had an idea that seal-skins were worth more than ten times what they were sold for on the London Market; and this without any expense, and the skins almost all destroyed in the flensing. When they left the fat, there was little to pay or trade for; this, however, they could not do, as they required it all for use through the winter. When a bear-skin was brought, though it was small, a telescope or a gun was asked for it. They are much like those who said, 'If one never asks, one never gets.' They all charged well for their goods, and had been accustomed to getting full value for seal-skins or for any other skins they ever took on board the whalers when they were there (Mutch, 1906: 488).

Many observers of recent Canadian Arctic history have suggested that the Inuit have been economically exploited by outsiders, from whalers through to free traders and the Hudson Bay Company. Captain Mutch's statement strongly implies that if exploitation did occur, it did not happen to naïve aboriginal peoples who did not understand the nature of an economic transaction.

The introduction of rifles that is mentioned by Mutch was to have long-term economic and ecological consequences for the Tununermiut and their environment. For one thing, it made them increasingly dependent on outsiders for supplies of ammunition, which obviously had to be replenished regularly. Also, the use of rifles made possible larger and more predictable, or regularized, kills, which in turn ensured more plentiful meat. This meant that for the first time, perhaps, the people had a surplus of food, as men killed more animals than were needed for the survival of their families. Excess meat was used to feed the dogs. Traditionally, only small dog teams of one, two, or three animals had been kept, but it was now possible to maintain larger teams. This had two effects, the first of which was to allow hunters to extend their individual hunting territories. Larger teams meant that greater distances could be covered on the hunt. The other effect was that dogs began to be considered a status symbol; the larger his team, the higher the status of a hunter. This, I believe, created a type of vicious cycle in which more meat was needed to feed the dogs, and so the dependency on ammunition was reinforced. Of course a greater number of killings had an effect on the seal and caribou populations.

As I mentioned earlier, the increasing patterns of mutual relationships between Tununermiut and whalers were not limited to the economic realm alone, but extended into other areas of life. Crews were regularly given shore leave when ships were in the vicinity of Inuit bands, whether the ships were Scottish or American. As I hypothesized before, the Inuit must have made their typically keen observations of the men, and it is likely that many Inuit women exchanged sexual favours for items of hardware, tobacco, foodstuffs, with Inuit males often acting as "brokers." It is likely that not all such encounters were consensual, though; while it cannot be documented, it was probably at the times of these shore leaves that Inuit women first experienced sexual assault (being physically and forcibly taken by European or Canadian males without the consent of either themselves or their spouses).

To pass from the savage to the sublime, Inuit were often invited onboard ships to attend religious services, and while this must have been their first introduction to Christianity, it is unlikely that they had much understanding of its form or content. The captains of the ships that wintered in Arctic waters would invite local Inuit to participate with their crews in festive celebrations such as Christmas.

The Tununermiut, although in contact with the Scots, who were less inclined than their American counterparts to employ Inuit workers, nevertheless did provide services for the whalers and had close contact with them. By the end of the nineteenth century there had been contact not only with whalers working the waters around Pond Inlet or wintering there in its relatively protected environment, but also with whaling stations as far away as Repulse Bay. Occasionally the Tununermiut would carry mail between geographically widely separated whaling stations (Low, 1906: 58). The growing exposure to alien cultural practices and institutions inevitably took on intellectual and social qualities as well as the strictly economic.

Traditional healing among the Tununermiut, as with other Inuit, was carried out by shamans. The whalers provided the first non-traditional medical services for the people of the Pond Inlet area, although on an intermittent basis. There are numerous mentions in ships' logs of sick or injured Inuit being taken onboard for medical attention, and of ship doctors going ashore to administer treatment. In some emergency situations, the doctors travelled long distances to provide assistance. Captain Low, when he visited Pond Inlet in 1903, described large whale-boats going from shore to ship filled with Inuit suffering from what he diagnosed as a form of typhoid-pneumonia.

The whaling industry, then, and the men who worked the ships that serviced it, had a permanent impact on the lives of the Tununermiut of Pond Inlet, and the eastern Arctic Inuit in general. It was the whalers who gave these Inuit their first systematic look at a world-view and cultural practices that would impinge on their own lives from that time on. Their later relations with representatives of that alien world were probably determined in no small way by the impressions gained and the relationships formed during the whaling period. I believe that Arctic historians and anthropologists have not paid enough attention to that period in their efforts to understand the Inuit's later strategies for coping with change. One reason for this, of course, has been a paucity of information, and perhaps a mistrust of the information that is available. The whalers were exploiters of a resource, and not observers of responses to their own presence among the Inuit. Their recorded descriptions of Inuit were relatively static, by which I mean that they described them as if they were museum pieces caught by a still camera. Although there was some attempt at objectivity, the intellectual climate of Europe and Canada at the time was such that there was little understanding of the nature of cultures and cultural variation, and racist thinking was prevalent. Both were reflected in the impressionistic records of the captains of ships and the few casually kept diaries that survive. Nevertheless, it is a worthwhile exercise to work through the documents, many of which are available in the National Archives in Ottawa. This period of Inuit contact with the outside world is too important to be forgotten.

Whatever influence the whalers had on the eastern Inuit, their presence was always peripatetic. While they often wintered in areas such as that around Pond Inlet, populated with nomadic Inuit, they did not establish any permanent settlements. The Inuit watched them come and go over the seasons.

BECOMING CANADIANS

The social and cultural changes that occurred among the Tununermiut in the second half of this century were products of the Canadian federal government. Although the claiming of the Arctic islands for Canada had little initial impact on the Inuit, by the time the period with which we are most concerned arrived, there had been considerable governmental involvement with them. The whaling industry peaked at the turn of the century and then began a rapid waning. From about that time, outside influences on the Tununermiut and other Inuit of the high Arctic were to come from Canada rather than Scotland or the United States. This influence, initially sporadic, would soon become continual and year-round.

The beginning of the Tununermiut's year-round contact with southern Canadians came about through a set of almost accidental circumstances. The cooper (barrel maker) of a Scottish whaling ship reported on his return home in 1892 that placer gold was abundant in the Pond Inlet area, and that it was regularly used by the Inuit as a trade item (Anonymous, unpublished article). On learning of the rumour, not wishing to lose this resource to foreign interests, the Canadian government commissioned Captain Joseph Bernier to travel north to investigate it. Captain Bernier and his ship, the *Minnie Maud*, were to become legends in eastern Arctic history. Bernier found no basis for the rumour, but, being something of an entrepreneur, while he was anchored at the site that was to become Pond Inlet he established a permanent trading post, the first in the area. In spite of his report denying the rumour, like most rumours this one was slow to die, and the lure of gold continued to captivate people in the south. Soon after, Bernier's trading post was purchased by the Arctic Gold Exploration Company, which had dual interests in fur trading and gold exploration. From the establishment of the post onward, the Tununermiut were to have continuous year-round exposure to Canadian influences. The outsiders had come to stay once and for all.

In 1906, in a sense as a harbinger to more contemporary concerns, the Government of Canada became concerned with the activities of foreign ships in Canadian Arctic waters. The government objected, not to the presence of these ships, but to the fact that they were not paying customs duties. In any event, as a result the federal government decided to play a more active role in the administration of its northern territories. On the basis of an order-in-council of 1906, Captain Bernier was once again commissioned to lead an expedition into the Arctic regions, this time with a broader mandate. His orders were to tour the eastern Arctic zones claimed by Canada with the purpose of "asserting Canadian sovereignty in the arctic regions which are territory of this Dominion by right of cession made to Canada by the Imperial Government" (Bernier, 1909: intro. n.p). This was truly a historic voyage, which laid the basis for all contemporary claims to Canadian sovereignty in its eastern Arctic lands and waters, and to the resources found within them.

Bernier's voyage was not the beginning of Canadian political involvement in its Arctic regions, however, but rather the culmination of several previous developments in areas other than the eastern. Earlier the government had decided to establish permanent stations in more southern parts of its Arctic territories for, in particular, the collection of customs from American whalers and, more generally, to administer and enforce Canadian law among the native peoples. In the high Arctic, though, whalers had continued to hunt without paying custom duties. Farther west, several North West Mounted Police outposts had been established in the more heavily populated regions of that territory, but they had had little effect on the activities of the whalers working high eastern waters, or on the local Inuit. In 1903, three years before Bernier's expedition, Superintendent J.D. Moodie, who had been appointed acting commissioner of the still largely unorganized Northwest Territories, sailed north with Captain Low on the C.G.S. *Neptune* to try to set these matters straight.

Superintendent Moodie's orders had been to impress upon both Inuit and non-Inuit residents and interlopers that they now resided on Canadian soil, and were therefore subject to Canadian laws. He was not to introduce Canadian law enforcement harshly, but persuade the people with whom he came into contact of their reciprocal obligations to Canada and Canadian society, of which they were, in at least a formal sense, now a part (Van Norman, 1951: 111).

It is extremely unlikely that the voyage of the *Neptune* had much impact on the consciousness or behaviour of the Inuit encountered on the expedition. I have been unable to discover what methods were used to communicate their new status to the people. Interpreters must have been used to overcome the linguistic barrier; but the Inuit, upon hearing that they were now part of an alien and to them probably incomprehensible political structure, would, I would guess, have listened politely and then filed the episode as one more example of the strange ways of the increasingly prevalent intruders in their lands. The Inuit had their own techniques for dealing with social disorder, their own definitions of what constituted socially unacceptable behaviour, and, however flexible and indeed unstructured it may have appeared to be to outsiders, their own form of political organization. My informants of sixty years later still had difficulty comprehending the idea of Canada as a vast nation with its political headquarters in Ottawa. How much more difficult it must have been for their fathers and grandfathers who encountered Superintendent Moodie and his political and legal messages. They went right on behaving as they had done for centuries, unmindful of whether or not they were in violation of Canadian laws, whatever those may have been, and decreasingly, whalers from Scotland continued to hunt in the eastern Arctic waters.

(On this topic of insularity, I am reminded of the reaction of my informants in 1964 to the assassination of John F. Kennedy. By chance I heard a radio broadcast from Dallas describing the tragedy. I tried to explain to the people around me what had happened, but they had considerable difficulty understanding the position and power of a president. Some wanted to know if Washington, DC, was a settlement like Pond Inlet. In another case, in responses to an item on a questionnaire administered to all adults in the area later that year and designed to reveal perceptions of Canadian law and government, the majority were unable to list three Canadian laws other than game ordinances.)

It was these realities that probably led to the 1906 order-in-council directing Captain Bernier to attempt to bring the northern regions of Canada under direct government supervision and to reinforce Canadian sovereignty. On his expedition of reclamation, Bernier had extensive contact with the Tununermiut. He had no sooner laid anchor outside Albert Harbour, eighteen miles northeast of the present settlement of Pond Inlet, than he sent out notices to all whalers operating in the area informing them of a new law requiring them to obtain whaling licenses to work in Canadian waters. On August 21, 1906, he claimed Bylot Island, located approximately twenty miles from Pond Inlet, for Canada and erected a cairn with the Canadian flag rooted in its top.

Bernier had planned to winter in Arctic Bay, some distance to the west of Pond Inlet, but finding no people in the area, returned to Albert Harbour, claiming several other islands for Canada while in transit. During the winter that followed there was considerable interaction between the ship's crew and the Tununermiut, who, for one thing, heard alien music for perhaps the first time when the ship's gramophone was played for them. According to Bernier, they were "amazed and amused at this music." (Bernier, 1909: 34) Many regularly attended religious services aboard ship, and on Christmas Day about 120 accepted an invitation to a Christmas meal of Canadian cuisine. Earlier, on November 9, when the Canadian flag had been hoisted at Pond Inlet and formal possession taken of Baffin Island, Captain Bernier had delivered a speech in which he told the assembled Inuit that they were Canadian citizens and were expected to live in peace with one another and to obey Canadian laws. Following the Christmas dinner he addressed them again, "telling them that they were Canadians and would be treated as such as long as they would do what was right" (Bernier, 1909: 39).

He seems to have been reasonably confident that the presence of his crew was having a salutary effect on the Tununermiut. After another shipboard celebration held on New Year's Day he recorded the following comments:

> The usual Sunday service was held ... quite a number of Eskimos were present. During the day we received the visits of many natives, who came to wish us the compliments of the season; we entertained them suitably for the occasion. They seem to be more assured than they were when we first came into the harbour, and they do not avoid us so much as they did then. Our way of living has evidently served as a good example to them, as they are not so wild and have better conduct all around. (Bernier, 1909)

Bernier seemed to believe, then, that he had established a good relationship with the local Inuit. He kept detailed notes in his journal of their economic involvement with traders and other outsiders, and the patterns of reciprocity established between the two populations. He notes, for example, that the Inuit traded furs, fresh meat, and narwhal tusks with both whalers and traders for tea, molasses, biscuits, sugar, tobacco, matches, knives, cooking utensils, ammunition, and clothing. These were not beads or "wampum," but trade items that the Inuit used in their daily lives in practical

Qamaniq struggles with his dogs, Aullativik, 1963.

and, in the instances of sugar and tobacco, unfortunate ways. One obvious consequence of these exchanges was the modification of the traditional Inuit dietary patterns. For the first time, carbohydrate in the form of raw sugar was part of the regular Inuit diet. This change was to have long-range effects on the morbidity of the people. I can recall awakening each morning, when I lived with a family on the land in 1964, to watch my Inuit hosts indulge in cups of tea, each sweetened by several spoonsful of sugar if it was available, and freshly rolled cigarettes, before climbing out of their sleeping robes. The pattern I witnessed had its roots in the whaling period a half century and more earlier. (The tea was not what one would be served in the Empress Hotel in Victoria. As it continued to be an expensive food item until the Tununermiut moved into the settlement, tea leaves were used over and over again. Each morning, and at tea breaks during the day, a handful of fresh leaves would be tossed into a beat-up kettle to revive the thick layer of white leaves that coated its bottom. The product was black, pungent, and, what was most important on tea breaks while on the trail, hot.) Tobacco, whether in plug form in the early days or, later as cigarettes, must certainly have contributed to the high incidence of tuberculosis among Canadian Inuit in this century.

Captain Bernier's admonitions about the observance of Canadian law may have had some temporary effect on the behaviour of the Tununermiut, for the only serious crime brought to his attention during the year spent at Albert Harbour was a shooting incident. A local Inuit called Snider was shot by a fellow hunter while both were out on a hunting trip. Snider died shortly after the incident, and Bernier considered holding an inquest, which, had it taken place, would have been the first court proceeding in the high eastern Arctic. However, he decided against, apparently because the accused was seriously ill for several months after the incident, and Snider, although asked before his death if he wished to do so, declined to place a charge against the man. This is, incidentally, one of several instances in which Captain Bernier demonstrated compassion for the Inuit, and some appreciation of their traditional techniques for dealing with disputes between individuals.

The historic voyage of the C.G.S. *Arctic* in some respects portended the end of the whaling period in the eastern Arctic. The activities of foreign and Canadian whalers alike had now come under government regulation, and this may have inhibited their activities, but more importantly, the industry had crested. The Industrial Revolution had provided cheap substitutes for whale byproducts such as oil, and women's clothing styles had changed, with whale-bone corsets no longer considered necessary undergarments. In the early years of this century the last whaling ships wintered near Pond Inlet, and soon even these disappeared. It is an open question how long the whale populations could have sustained the intense hunting that had taken place during the zenith of the industry.

During the first two decades of this century, therefore, the Tununermiut were formally citizens of Canada and had already experienced several decades of economic, social, and intellectual involvement with the outside world. They were economically dependent upon trade goods that had become standard fare in their diet and a central part of their hunting technology. These needs were met by the trading post originally established by Joseph Bernier and by occasional free traders who would spend a year or so trying to amass their personal fortunes by trading for furs and skins. On the other hand, with the absence of the whalers the Tununermiut were once again free to follow their own pursuits and to live a fairly traditional way of life, which they proceeded to do. But the influence of the whaling period was indelible, and, as I have argued, the consequences of more intensified and prolonged contacts with the outside world were based upon that influence.

A TRADING POST BECOMES A SETTLEMENT

Aside from the Bernier expedition of 1906, the first two decades of this century witnessed little direct government action or involvement in the central and eastern Arctic. Bernier himself made several other expeditions to various areas, claiming new lands for Canada and reasserting Canadian sovereignty, but in general this was a dormant period in the history of high Arctic colonialism. The Northwest Territories continued to be administered by the Royal North-West Mounted Police, with the comptroller of the force acting as territorial commissioner. New police departments were established in several settlements, but they were spread out from one another. It was not until a dramatic set of events occurred in the 1920s that a detachment was placed in Pond Inlet.

The Coming of the Bay

Possibly because of rumours of oil deposits, and in general an increased southern Canadian interest in northern resources such as oil, in 1920 the deputy minister of the Department of the Interior was appointed commissioner of the Northwest Territories (Flanagan, 1963: 37). From then on the concept of "northern development" began to become a reality, and federal interest in the Arctic gradually extended beyond mere policing of it. 1920 was also the year in which the Arctic Gold Exploration Company in Pond Inlet was sold to the Hudson Bay Company.

"The Bay," as the company came to be known throughout the Arctic, had taken over posts operated by free traders in several embryonic settlements. It began its operation in Pond Inlet in 1921, when the company ship *Baychimo* brought materials to stock and a man to staff the new post. With this development Pond Inlet entered a new phase in its history; there was now present in the tiny settlement the first of the four agencies that were to shape its future for several decades to come. The others — police, missionaries, and federal civil servants — would arrive later. As mentioned earlier, the traders who managed the HBC post were not interested in changing the lifestyles of the local Inuit, but their presence none-theless had unintended consequences. They wanted fox furs and seal skins, and to obtain them provided the trade goods on which the Tununermiut had become dependent, but it was in their own interest to keep the people "on the land," maintaining a fairly traditional life-style with hunting as its economic base.

One major effect of a trading post in Pond Inlet was to alter the residential and nomadic patterns of the Inuit, and this effect was accelerated by the HBC. The Tununermiut began to settle in semi-sedentary camps in order to be near the post, and increasingly to hunt in a radius around it. Also, for the first time, a few individuals found regular wage employment. It was company practice to hire at least one family to work at the trading post. Men would hunt for meat for the trader's dogteam, pack skins, and clerk in the post itself. Women would work as housekeepers for the traders and, in some instances, provide sexual services. (One of my key informants in 1964 was the offspring of a liaison between his mother and a trader, and his own wife had borne a child while, before her marriage, working as a housekeeper at the HBC post.) I have the impression, although I cannot verify it, that in the early days of the trading post men were hired not so much for their skill or industry as for the attractiveness of their wives. In any event, the experience of full-time employment by the traders was a new one for the Inuit.

A Killing Brings the Police and a Detachment

Throughout and following World War I, although the Canadian Arctic regions were under the formal administration of the Department of the Interior, the implementation of that administration was largely carried out in the field by the Royal Canadian Mounted Police (Lesage, 1955: 3). The number of police detachments increased, and an annual patrol by ship was initiated. In the high eastern Arctic in particular, the resident RCMP officer acted as the link between the Inuit and the Department of the Interior offices in Ottawa. The role of the police as administrators in this region was to be significant, and to continue for several decades. In 1923, two years after the HBC took over the trading post, the first police detachment was established in Pond Inlet.

That detachment might have been established even later, were it not for a sequence of quite dramatic events in the post-contact history of the Tununermiut. Because of the fascinating nature of these events (and also because of my own original research interests

RCMP detatchment. Pond Inlet, 1963.

in the legal acculturation of the Tununermiut), I will try to recon-
struct them in some detail. These are the events that surrounded
the well-known but poorly documented "Janes case."

Visitors to Pond Inlet, if they take the time to walk along the
beach outside of the settlement, may come across a small wooden
cross marking a grave (if it still stands). The grave is that of Robert
Janes, a Newfoundlander and free trader. It was the manner in
which he died, and events following it, that precipitated the establishment of an RCMP detachment at Pond Inlet.

Janes had been a second officer on an expedition made by
Joseph Bernier in 1910, which had visited Pond Inlet. A few years
later Janes decided to return to this area and attempt to make his
fortune as a free trader. He enlisted the financial backing of several
silent partners in Newfoundland. Several accounts of what happened to Janes are found in histories of the RCMP and local histories
of Pond Inlet, but there are discrepancies among these; the following is my attempt to distinguish fact from fiction. The story has
taken on legendary status in modern Arctic folklore.

Janes had left a wife behind in Newfoundland, but on his return
to Pond Inlet he took up residence with an Inuit woman — an
arrangement that, as mentioned earlier, was by no means unusual
in the early days of contact between Inuit and outsiders. The fact

that the woman already had a husband did not seem to bother Janes. There are suggestions in his diary that he had little respect for the Inuit, but he was able to overcome this prejudice enough to create what were for him lucrative trading relationships with them. During his first year he amassed a large collection of furs, and felt that his venture had been financially successful.

Originally, he had planned to return at the end of that year onboard the *Albert*, which would be bringing supplies north for the Pond Inlet trading post. Shortly before the ship was to arrive, he gave what remained of his trade goods to several local Inuit, since they had no more furs to trade and it would have been expensive to take the goods back with him.

When the *Albert* arrived, the captain refused to take him aboard. It is unclear whether this was because of a dispute Janes had with Henry Toke Munn, manager of the trading post, with whom Janes had not been on friendly terms, or because of an argument with the captain about the cost of his passage. In any event, Janes was forced to change his plans.

I have the impression, from reading Janes' diary, that he had spent most of the previous year living on the land and travelling with the Inuit. Perhaps the stress of this sort of life, with its isolation from his own cultural moorings, combined with that created by his dispute over his passage south, caused him to become temporarily mentally unbalanced. He was forced to remain for a second year, and his already negative feelings towards the Inuit seemed to assume an outright hostile cast. His behaviour towards them became abusive.

Janes' feelings toward the Inuit finally erupted: he attacked an older man with a knife, cutting his clothes but not injuring him seriously. The man was the father-in-law of the woman with whom Janes had been living; according to Wilfred Caron, a clerk at the trading post, the son had been angry about being cuckolded but was afraid of Janes, so his father had confronted the Newfoundlander. And so Janes had violated two basic legal norms of traditional Inuit society: unjustified attack on another person, and having sexual relations with a man's wife without his permission. Either, under customary law, might have led to a societal response, for they both constituted threats to the public good and to social order. A retaliative killing of the offender would have been a socially approved execution.

Janes had, then, become a threat to the Tununermiut. In time, he would threaten them openly and intentionally. When he had given away his remaining trade goods, while awaiting the arrival of the *Albert*, they had been accepted by the recipients as gifts. Generosity and the sharing of largesse were probably the foundations of traditional Inuit ethics. Acts of generosity did not necessarily carry with them the right to demand reciprocity at a future date. Believing that he would be leaving the area shortly, Janes had not made any demands that the "gifts" be repaid in the future with furs and skins, and the beneficiaries of his gifts did not feel under any obligation to him.

During the second year of his stay, or the year of his exile, having nothing left to trade himself, he approached those Inuit who had been recipients of his benevolence the year before and asked for skins and furs without payment, claiming that he had earlier extended credit to them. His logic was not acceptable to them, and his hostile behaviour towards them had alienated them. Instead, they told him that they would receive full payment for their skins at either Cape Fullerton or the trading post at Pond Inlet, and intended to take them to one or the other. They needed goods such as flour, tea, and ammunition, and so were going to take their business to where they could acquire them.

The estranged relations between Janes and the Tununermiut were conducive to a dramatic confrontation, and the last entry in Janes' diary describes the one that developed.

> Light N.E. wind fine and clear. All natives hunting today, few got seals. Two paid me for goods delivered last year, and other fellow whom I interviewed told me he had no foxes but I told him I know better and he had better pay up if not I would shoot his and the other dogs as sure as the sun rises, and I will too. I guess they will pay up later and save trouble. I have given myself a lot of trouble by issuing these fellows credit. It is a bad policy in this land. (National Archives of Canada, Ottawa)

The entry was dated Saturday, March 14, 1920, and he probably died the following day or soon after. If he had been a danger to the social order before, he became even more of one by his threats. The dogs of the Tununermiut had taken on new importance since the whaling days, both as status symbols and as contributors to hunting success. Men competed with one another using their teams. Also, they were beginning to enter the contact-traditional period, characterized by a more sedentary life in fairly permanent camps located within commuting distance of the trading post at Pond Inlet. With diminished game resources in the immediate area,

Hunter prepares his sled. Aullativik, 1963.

brought about by hunting with rifles rather than harpoons, and the need for larger supplies of meat to feed their dogs, men hunted farther and farther afield. For this, large teams were a necessity. A threat to their dogs was to be taken seriously. It is possible that the Tununermiut feared that after Janes had killed the dogs, he might then begin to kill them.

When the last entry in his diary was recorded, Janes had been camping at Cape Crawford, near the present settlement of Arctic Bay. He was trying to reach Chesterfield Inlet, from where he hoped to find transportation south. According to testimony given by local Inuit at the trial, on March 15 or soon after Janes' assistant went hunting, taking with him Janes' own rifle. Several Inuit families were camped nearby, among them the young man whose wife was living with Janes, along with two of his close friends. It was claimed at the trial that several meetings were held to determine how to deal with the threats Janes had made. The final conclusion was that he should be executed. Since the husband, Nookudlah, was the one most wronged by Janes, he was appointed executioner.

While his assistant was away, and he was without a rifle to defend himself, Janes was called from his tent by one of Nookudlah's friends, and when he stepped outside Nookudlah fired three shots at him. Possibly out of fear of actually killing an outsider, however justified, Nookudlah only wounded him. Later that day Nookudlah attacked Janes again, and Janes died as a result of his wounds.

At the time of these events, the Tununermiut had been under the formal jurisdiction of Canadian law for over fifty years. The extent of their awareness of it is that, after killing Janes, Nookudlah buried his body under a cairn of rocks, collected his belongings, and delivered them to Wilfred Caron at the Pond Inlet trading post. He explained to Caron what he had done, and what had provoked his actions. It is doubtful that he was in any respect "turning himself in" to a representative of the society of the outsiders. Rather, it seems that he was merely providing an explanation for a sequence of events that, while regrettable, had terminated in a necessary and wholly justified execution under Inuit customary law.

Caron apparently accepted the explanation and let the matter drop. Nothing further developed in the case until several months later, when Janes' wife back in Newfoundland, with the support of his parents, decided to initiate an enquiry into the whereabouts of her husband and requested an investigation by the RCMP. In response to that request and journalistic pressure, Commissioner A. Bowen Perry instructed Sergeant Alfred Herbert Joy to proceed to Pond Inlet with the dual directives of uncovering the fate of Janes and establishing an RCMP detachment at Pond Inlet. The formal instructions given Sergeant Joy are revealing of the multitude of activities performed by police in the Canadian Arctic of the time:

A detachment is to be established at Pond Inlet, Baffin Island, and you have been selected to take charge of it. You have been appointed a justice of the peace in the Northwest Territories, in which Baffin Island is situated, a coroner, a special officer of the customs, and a postmaster of a post office located at Pond Inlet. Your general duty is to enforce law and order in all the district tributary to Pond Inlet, and the authority given you as justice of the peace and coroner will enable you to deal with most cases which may arise of an infraction of the law.

As a special officer of the customs, it will be your duty to enforce the customs laws and carry out the detailed instructions issued you by the Customs Department. As postmaster at Pond Inlet, it will be your duty to carry on these duties in accordance with the post office regulations.

Your special attention is directed to an alleged murder of a Mr. Janes, by an Eskimo, and you are directed to make a thorough enquiry into this murder, and take such steps as are required to bring the guilty parties to justice. Should you find that there is a *prima facie* case against any person or persons, it will be your duty, if it is clearly established, to take the accused into custody and hold him pending instructions from headquarters.

Arrangements are made for your board and lodging with the Hudson's Bay Company post at Pond Inlet. Although you are indebted to the Hudson's Bay Company for your transportation and board and lodging, and many other necessary requirements, still you must bear in mind that you are a servant of the Government, and must deal with all trading companies exactly on an equal footing.

I rely on your good judgement and previous experience to carry out your important duties with credit to yourself and to the satisfaction of headquarters.

[signed] A. Bowen Perry, *Commissioner*

(*Report of the Royal Canadian Mounted Police*, 1922: 20-21)

Sergeant Joy arrived at Pond Inlet on August 30, 1921, aboard the HBC supply ship *Baychimo*. On December 7 he left for Cape Crawford, and a fortnight later, on exhuming Janes' body, found "two bullet holes and incontestable evidence that the deceased had come to his end by violence" (Official RCMP report quoted in Steele, n.d.: 228). After transporting the decomposed remains back to Pond Inlet, a distance of some two hundred miles, he called for a coroner's inquest. Three traders performed jury duty at the inquest. On February 11 they returned a verdict of murder against Nookudlah, and ruled that two other men were accomplices who had aided and abetted him.

When this judgement was communicated to RCMP headquarters in Ottawa, the authorities decided to make an example of the case. Arrangements were made to conduct a full-scale formal trial in Pond Inlet. In July 1923 the C.G.S. *Arctic* left Montreal for the northern settlement carrying Judge L.A. Rivert; Leopold Tellier, who was to act as defense counsel; F.X. Biron, a clerk of the court; Inspector C.E. Wilcox of the RCMP; and several non-commissioned officers and constables. They arrived at Pond Inlet on August 21, and four days later the court opened at the newly established police detachment. A jury had been selected from members of the crew of the *Arctic*. Several Inuit attended. The final disposition found

Nookudlah guilty of manslaughter, and he was sentenced to ten years' imprisonment in Stony Mountain penitentiary in Manitoba. The second man, Oo-roo-re-ung-nak (as his name was spelled in the trial proceedings), was also convicted of manslaughter, but on the basis of a recommendation for clemency he was sentenced to two years' hard labour, to be served in Pond Inlet. The third man, Ah-tee-tah, was acquitted (Annual Report of the RCMP, 1924: 33). I am not certain, but I believe that Nookudlah was the first Inuit to be sentenced to a Canadian federal penitentiary.

It seems that the court tried to view the case in the light of the fact that the Inuit of the area had had little formal experience with Canadian law, but also, the members of the court sought to make a lasting impression. Inspector Wilcox's final report, which I quote at length because I consider it to be an extremely interesting and revealing statement of the time, indicates that the court was satisfied that both aims had been accomplished.

This trial was conducted throughout strictly in accordance with the Rules and Regulations of the force, and with all the decorum of a Supreme Court in civilization.

The counsel for the defence in his plea for the accused pointed out the weakness of the evidence against Ah-tee-tah, and urged that he be discharged. He pleaded that the life of the Eskimos, their ignorance of the laws of civilization, and the provocation given them by Janes and be taken into consideration by the jury in arriving at their verdict.

... The counsel for the Crown pressed for a conviction of the three accused, and stated that in civilization he would ask for a verdict of murder, but taking into consideration the ignorance of the prisoners, he only asked for a verdict of manslaughter. He informed the jury that they could, if they desired, recommend the accused to the clemency of the court.

... It was apparent that the trial had been a severe strain on the accused, for they looked quite unwell at the termination. The effects of the sentence, I believe, will have a more beneficial effect than a sentence of death. The prisoner Nookudlah was led away immediately after the sentence was passed, to the ship, through a gazing crowd of his own people, without being given a chance to communicate with any of them. It is hardly possible that a native with the prestige that Nookudlah must have had with the other Eskimos at the time he killed Janes could have been subjected to greater humiliation than to be led away directly under the eyes of not less than one hundred of his relatives and friends.

After the termination of the trial, the judge addressed the entire Eskimo population outside the detachment, telling what they had to expect from the representatives of the Government, that they could expect kindness and protection from the police if they behaved well, but if they committed any crime, they could expect to be punished. They all immediately afterwards joined in three generous cheers for the judge.

(Report of Inspector C.E. Wilcox, quoted in *Report of the Royal Canadian Mounted Police*, 1924: 33-34)

Nookudlah was to serve only part of his sentence at Stony Mountain. His release came about after a plea for clemency was made on his behalf by Captain Joseph Bernier, who had learned that the prisoner was suffering from acute tuberculosis. Seriously ill, Nookudlah returned to Pond Inlet, where he died on December 5, 1925. He and his comrades were remembered by the older Tununermiut in the 1960s, and referred to as strong, able men, who had actually assisted Sergeant Joy when he was bringing them in to stand trial by hunting for him and keeping him alive during a severe storm. With considerable pride one informant told me that Ah-tee-tah was his grandfather. The story of the killing and its aftermath spread quickly through the informal communication networks in the eastern Arctic, but my impression has been that it was interpreted in traditional Inuit terms, and that little blame was attached to the three men involved. It had been, for them, a just execution.

Even without the legendary Janes case, however, Pond Inlet was destined to have its own permanent RCMP detachment because of its strategic position on the northern tip of Baffin Island, located approximately halfway between the settlements of Arctic Bay and Clyde River. It was established in 1922 and initially staffed by Sergeant Joy, a corporal, and two constables. Pond Inlet now had two of the three agencies that dominated almost all Canadian Arctic settlements before the intrusion of the Department of Northern Affairs decades later, and it was soon to receive the third.

The Coming of the Church

The first active suggestion that a mission should be established at Pond Inlet, and that the Tununermiut might be in need of Christian influence, came from a trader. Although he was a Protestant himself, earlier efforts to interest members of his own denomination had failed, and so he turned to Roman Catholics. He had met the famed Monseigneur Turquetial while both were passengers on the HBC ship *Nascopie*, and had later written to him to suggest that "only religion could make the Eskimos good hunters, men of action, and honest enough to pay their debts" (Morice, 1943: 173). His request to the Monseigneur that a mission be established in Pond Inlet, made in 1923, received an enthusiastic reply, but not until 1927 did preparations begin. In September 1929, Father Prime Girard arrived at Pond Inlet, accompanied by Father Étienne Bazin. They were to build the Sacred Heart Mission and to provide the Tununermiut with the Christian message. The comments of the trader, which initiated this development, were probably typical of the attitudes of outsiders towards the Inuit during that period. Fortunately, they were counterbalanced by the attitudes of individuals such as Joseph Bernier and Wilfred Caron. The thought that the Inuit had to "become" good hunters and men of action is ludicrous in the extreme. If they did not "pay their debts" it was likely because traders often extended credit to them, and, as in the case of Janes and his extra trade goods, credit was interpreted in traditional terms. Certainly the traders did little to explain the fundamentals of a cash economy to the Inuit.

This was, of course, not the first encounter the Tununermiut had had with Christianity, for, as we have seen, decades before they had attended church services onboard whaling and exploration ships. Also, in 1927, two years before the mission was established, two converted Inuit from Chesterfield Inlet had migrated to the Pond Inlet area. It is likely that members of these families did some proselytizing on their own, and acted as lay missionaries. To anticipate a later discussion: converted Inuit usually accepted Christianity with considerable zeal, and with the enthusiasm of the new convert often worked to bring others over to their new beliefs. In any event, in 1929 twenty-two Inuit living near Pond Inlet were baptized into the Roman Catholic faith, and eight of these were admitted to their first communion (Morice, 1943: 174).

During this same period the Anglican church was gradually extending its influence into the north and northeast regions of the Arctic, and in 1929 the Reverend Harold Duncan established the first Anglican mission in Pond Inlet. I believe that plans to open the Catholic mission were afoot before similar ones were made by Anglicans, but it is significant that both missions opened their doors in the same year. Ever since, Pond Inlet has had two missions representing the two major missionary movements in the Canadian Arctic. Rivalry between the two was long a characteristic of the settlement and on occasion erupted into open displays of hostility, but today there is an amicable relationship between the two missions. Statistically, the Anglicans seem to have won the long battle for the souls of the Tununermiut, the majority of whom are affiliated with it.

By 1930, then, Pond Inlet had for better or worse acquired all of the components of the triad that was to become the structural base for almost all Canadian Arctic settlements. For the next two decades it would remain a fairly stable and static community, and the Tununermiut would settle into the contact-traditional life-style, living in semi-permanent camps located within commuting distance of the settlement. They would experience increasing dependency on and involvement in the institutions of the outside world, while also retaining many characteristics of the social and cultural worlds of their forefathers.

On December 16, 1953, however, a change occurred in the administration of the settlement, one that was to have a dramatic effect on the people still living on the land, as well as on the settlement itself. The federal government established the Department of Northern Affairs and National Resources (DNANR) (Flanagan, 1963: 69), which was to take over the operations of the Department of the Interior in the Northwest Territories. From 1953 on, the government would be far more involved in northern resource development and in the administration of the native peoples of the territories, both Indian and Inuit.

During the winter of 1955–56, six Northern Service Officers (NSOs) were appointed to "coordinate field activities and supervise development in various remote areas" (Flanagan, 1963). They were to work in the field, and would automatically become the senior ranking civil servants in any settlements to which they were sent. Until that time, that status had been reserved for RCMP officers.

The first NSO was stationed in Pond Inlet in 1959, and in 1960 a school was built in the settlement. It was to be staffed by DNANR teachers, and the following March the first teacher arrived. The federal day school in Pond Inlet was officially opened on March 21, 1961; ten Tununermiut then had to contend not only with Euro-Canadian police, missionaries, traders, and administration, but also with formal Euro-Canadian education.

By 1961, the structure of the permanent settlement of Pond Inlet had been formed. Two years later, I first arrived in Pond Inlet. My attention was primarily directed at camp life, but I also spent time living in the settlement, or visiting it regularly while I lived on the land. It was a fascinating time for anyone interested in the dynamics of inter-agency co-operation and conflict, for the new DNANR operation had shaken up the settlement in several ways, if only by its increasing massiveness in relationship to the smaller agencies of the established triad. It was in many respects perceived as a threat by the traders, missionaries, and police. We shall return to the settlement and to the southern agencies that maintained outposts in it later, after looking at camp life of the early 1960s. It was a way of life that was soon to disappear, and the policy and procedures of the DNANR were largely responsible.

CAMP LIFE IN THE

CONTACT-TRADITIONAL PERIOD

During my first year of residence with them, approximately 280 Tununermiut lived in the vicinity of Pond Inlet. Ever since Captain Bernier established the first trading post, a few had lived in the settlement itself, and that number had increased over time as the settlement grew, but when I first encountered the Tununermiut the vast majority still lived on the land. These "land" people were the hunters and their families who inhabited seven camps ranging in distance from eight to more than a hundred miles from Pond Inlet.

The camp people were traditionalists in many respects, still dependent on hunting for most of their food, speaking Inuktitut in their homes, maintaining a fairly conventional Inuit family structure, and, I am convinced, believing that they were living much as Inuit had lived for centuries. In psychological identity, they were in fact Inuit. But at the same time, their life-style was not that of their ancestors, and this was true not only because of technological change. True, they had outboard-motor-powered boats instead of kayaks and used rifles rather than harpoons, but they also ate bannock as a staple and attended Christian church services almost every Sunday morning. They were, then, firmly entrenched in the contact-traditional period described earlier. However, as I tried to illustrate in the last chapter, the process leading to this period had been slow and gradual, occurring over a time span of one hundred years or more, and it did not totally obliterate all features of the traditional culture.

The Tununermiut of 1963–64 had incorporated, on a selective basis, elements of the alien culture to which they had increasingly been exposed, but to a large extent this had been done pragmatically. I suggest that it was precisely because they continued to live on the land, and indeed had been encouraged to do so by the traders, police, and missionaries, that they were able to retain some conscious control over the degree to which they were influenced

Table 1: Inuit households in Pond Inlet, NWT, and Surrounding Camps, 1963

Camp	Households
Nallua	4
Qaurnak	6
Aullativik	5
Quimivvik	5
Illukisaat	3
Ippiarjuk	5
Igarguak	13
Pond Inlet	15
Total	56

by the alien forms. As I mentioned earlier, the traders wanted their furs and so encouraged a hunting economy. The police believed that if people were kept on the land they would be less likely to fall prey to alcohol and its attendant antisocial and illegal behaviour. The police were also, until the DNANR arrived, responsible for doling out welfare, and they assumed that continued reliance on a hunting economy would deter dependence on welfare. The missionaries, according to several with whom I held interviews, feared that within the settlement the Tununermiut would be influenced by secularization, with a concomitant increase in immorality and adoption of non-Christian behaviour patterns. During this period, the Tununermiut themselves valued camp life, and with few exceptions were not drawn to the settlement other than for trading and occasional visiting.

So, the Tununermiut of that period did live in a fairly traditional way, even with the borrowed technology: they respected traditional patterns of hospitality and sharing, spoke their own language almost exclusively, and in general identified psychologically as Inuit. Most of them lived in the outlying camps.

Primarily as a means of giving men adequate territory for successful hunting, the number of families in each camp was quite small, averaging six households each and with large distances separating them. By "household" I mean separate residences that housed a nuclear family (or a husband and wife and unmarried children), or an elderly couple, or, in some instances, a widow or widower with or without unmarried children (See Table 1). In a few cases aged parents lived with their married children, but more commonly they either had their own residences or had moved into the settlement where they had been given government-subsidized housing. If they lived alone in camps, they were provided for by their married sons or sons-in-law.

In Aullativik, the camp in which I lived for most of that first year, there were five households, all connected with one another through ties of kinship. Many of the statements I make in this chapter are really generalizations based upon what I observed during the nine months I lived with the Aullativikmiut. However, I also spent short periods of time in other camps, either on visits when accompanying Aullativikmiut on hunting trips, or on excursions of my own. The latter were made only after I had learned to handle a dog team fairly proficiently and with some measure of confidence.

Aullativik in Summer and Winter

The high degree of mobility between camps in the 1960s gives me some assurance that my generalizations are ethnographically valid, and that Aullativik was well within the parameters of typical camp structure. Visiting between camps, despite the distances between them, was a regular event, although most commonly done by men out on hunting expeditions, without the company of spouses and young children. Also, even though residence in a particular camp was usually, if not always, contingent upon the individual family's having ties of kinship with at least one family already resident in it, people did move back and forth between camps. This in part reflected the traditional Inuit pattern of seasonal fission and fusion. One could be a Qimivvikmiut one year and an Aullativikmiut the next. Some of the people from "my" camp spent the spring months in other camps or out on their own, and one family who had been living in the settlement joined us. Along with this fluidity, however, there was a fair degree of residential stability during the contact-traditional period.

Unfortunately, my data do not permit me to venture claims about the fission and fusion processes practised in that period. I do have confidence that Aullativik was typical of other Tununermiut camps, and that the camps that surrounded Pond Inlet in 1963–64 were probably similar in most respects to Inuit camps across Arctic Canada. But for present purposes, the important

Family covering winterhouse with summer tent. Aullativik, 1963.

point is that the life of the contact-traditional camp was one shared by most Tununermiut, and it is that life which was so abruptly dislodged in the latter part of the 1960s.

During the contact-traditional period the Aullativikmiut, like other Tununermiut, maintained two camps, one for summer and the other for winter, and they were both strategically placed. When I first arrived to stay with them, they were still living in the summer camp, but two weeks later we moved to Aullativik, the winter camp on Curry Island. It was nestled in front of a long, high hill and protected from winter winds by tall mountains on either side and by the jagged cliffs of Baffin Island, which were only a mile or so across the water. The summer camp was being used for the first time, and when we left two weeks after my arrival, it would be abandoned permanently. It was a good location for the men to go off on hunting trips, and at first glance seemed to be protected by high rocks, but the winds that drove across it from Eclipse Sound, onto which it faced, were unbearable for the women and children. Also, the fresh water supply provided by a small glacial stream was totally inadequate for the families living there. I did not have proper Arctic clothing at the time, and was to spend the two weeks at that camp shivering, sick at times from the new diet to which I was adjusting, and extremely miserable. The water quality may have been a factor as well. More than once, as I also felt the frustrations of being a monolingual English speaker living among monolingual speakers of Inuktitut, I wondered in my solitary walks whatever had possessed me to want to do field work in an Inuit camp on northern Baffin Island. One consolation was that there were no dogs present, so one could defecate behind rocks without having to carry a club to fend them off. They had been left on Curry Island, where they were periodically fed by the men of the camp.

I also experienced a sense of humiliation when we finally, and earlier than was normal, broke camp and moved to Aullativik. The men made the trip in their small, outboard-driven boats and canoes, while I was escorted in the large whale boat with the women and children. This experience was not only humiliating, but more positively, taught me my first lesson in Arctic humility. I may have been near to earning a doctorate at an Ivy League university, but in that environment, and in an Inuit camp, all of my knowledge and experience were of little value to me, and the Inuit males recognized this. I had asked Jimmy Muckpah to teach me to live as an Inuit, and he was taking that task seriously. I was beginning my life among the people with the status of a child, and I soon learned how appropriate that was. The men usually stood up while running their boats, with a hand on the throttle of the "kicker," as outboard motors were called, and the dramatic effect of these men as their boats bounced on the waves accentuated the contrast with my own position, huddling for warmth in a boat filled with women and children. Any thoughts I had developed of myself as an adult male of the 1960s were put to a harsh test on the day of the move to Aullativik.

When the Aullativikmiut had abandoned their winter camp the previous spring, individual households had gone off in separate directions for a few weeks, taking advantage of the good hunting, before regrouping at the summer camp. There were five tents in that summer camp in the summer of 1963, just as there were five houses at Aullativik. Because of the continual high winds that buffeted the area, the tents were laid out in relationship to one another in a way that provided maximum protection, rather than in an orderly manner side by side along the waterfront, as was the more typical pattern for a Tununermiut camp.

The tents were of white canvas and had been made by the women of the households. Within each tent, caribou hides covered the rear half, with one facing down and the other reversed, hairs facing up, an arrangement that made best use of the excellent insulating qualities of caribou hide — each hair is tubular, and retains warmth. The hides, in turn, were covered with either a cloth or a blanket. This was the sleeping area. All members of a family slept side by side, with parents at one side and beside them the youngest child, at times an infant. The other children slept on the other side in stepladder fashion, all with their feet to the rear of the tent and heads pointed to the entrance and, had the tents been laid out in a conventional pattern, the sea. Heat in the tent was provided by the soapstone *kudlik*, a heavy, half-moon-shaped, shallow bowl in which melted seal fat was burned. The moss wick had to be tended hourly, and always went out soon after the woman of the household had gone to sleep at night. Other warmth came from the body heat of the occupants. I was never warm in the day during the two weeks I lived in Jimmy Muckpah's tent before we moved to Aullativik, but then, my body chemistry had not yet adapted to the constant just-above-freezing temperatures. At night, I slept beside the children in two sleeping bags, one inside the other, and would dread the mornings. The Inuit slept under blankets that had been purchased at the HBC post in Pond Inlet, and quilts made by the women. Each of the families owned at least one primus stove, but because of the cost of coal oil these were used only for cooking, and even then only infrequently. The men would take them along on hunting trips to make tea. In some of the tents stood a four-foot-high tripod from which would be suspended the pan in which bannock was prepared.

As mentioned before, when I arrived at the camp the dogs of the Aullativikmiut were being kept across the inlet on Curry Island, but when dogs were present in a camp they usually huddled around the tent of their owners, growling menacingly at passers-by and, whenever I was about, standing ready to follow me when I went behind rocks to see to bodily functions. The half-wild dogs were almost always hungry, and would eat human feces along with anything else they could find. Seal skins in various stages of preparation were usually seen around tents, either strung tight across drying frames or slung over guide ropes. After the men had cut the hide off a seal carcass, it became the women's responsibility. After flensing it of the fat, they strung it onto a wooden frame, where it would remain for several days until the oils had seeped out of it, to be scraped off by the women. The Tununermiut did no tanning, so the skins were now rolled up ready to be taken to market. Occasionally the caribou sleeping robes would be hanging outside houses to air dry, if infants or small children had accidentally urinated on them.

Along the shoreline would be found a couple of seal carcasses

Winter camp of Aullativikmiut, 1963.

stripped of meat, drums filled with gasoline for the outboards, the
boats of hunters home from the hunt, and perhaps a fish net laid
out on the ground for repairs, but otherwise the ground around
the tents was bare. During that period the Tununermiut had few
material possessions, and most of what they did have could be kept
in their tents. (An inventory of items I found in Aullativikmiut
homes will be given later.) In general, except for the arrangement
of the tents, the scene I have described was very similar to what
was to be found at the winter camp, other than for sleds, which
had been left that summer on Curry Island with the dogs.

Because the winter camp of Aullativik was the opposite of the
summer camp of 1963 in terms of providing protection from the
elements, houses in the former were stretched out in a row along
the waterfront in conventional Tununermiut fashion. When
Tununermiut returned from their summer camps they would normally continue to live in tents for a week or two while making
necessary repairs to their houses. In the summer of 1963 the Aullativikmiut had originally planned to abandon Aullativik, which had
been used for approximately forty years, and to locate at a new
winter spot, but later changed their minds and returned for one
last year. I don't know how much my own presence, and their
concern for my well-being, influenced this change in plans, but, in

any event, we did return to Aullativik, and I was pleased that we did. Despite the accumulated debris of decades of residence that surrounded the houses and the waterfront, the camp was located in an idyllic setting. Because of the extensive repairs needed to put the houses in liveable condition, we remained in the tents for several weeks that year, while the temperatures dropped lower and lower.

When the interiors and exteriors of the houses had been repaired as well as possible, given the meagre supply of building materials, the people took occupancy. Arniatsiark, the camp headman and oldest male, lived in one house with his wife and unmarried children. On one side of his house was that of Kadloo, the first cousin of Jimmy Muckpah, who was the husband of one of Arniatsiark's daughters. (The previous year, Kadloo had wintered at Igloolik, where his wife's family lived, and his Aullativik house had been occupied by Arniatsiark's youngest married son. The son had vacated the camp to take up residence in Pond Inlet, where he had secured a job.) On the other side, and in the central building in the camp, lived Atagootung, Jimmy's widowed mother and one of the oldest living Inuit in the area. With her lived her adopted daughter, a girl in her early teens. The elderly matriarch often passed her time during my stay by telling me obscene stories accompanied by adroit manipulation of string figures she worked in her arthritic hands, and she often teased me by inviting me to live with her and her daughter, since she was without a man of her own. Next to her was the house of her son, Jimmy Muckpah, and his wife, Elisapee, the daughter of Arniatsiark. Beside them was the home of Qamanig and his family.

The winter houses at Aullativik were basically variations on the traditional Thule houses of sod and whale bone that the Tununermiut had lived in until the early decades of this century. The remains of a few old Thule houses could still be found a few miles outside Pond Inlet. These had been excavated by Therkel Matthiassen and his crew when they accompanied Knud Rasmussen on the Fifth Thule Expedition from Greenland to Alaska in the 1920s. The Aullativikmiut houses were one-room, as were virtually all Tununermiut houses of the 1960s, although there were a few two- and even three-room houses in a couple of camps. I will describe the houses and their contents in some detail both because accommodation has always been of such extreme importance to the Inuit, and also because it will give a picture of their material acculturation and the ways in which they modified traditional forms to accommodate newly available materials.

The typical floor plan was much like that found in the summer tents, with some elaborations. The sleeping area dominated the interior, often taking up more than half of the floor space. In each house a low entrance faced out onto the water, with a small, square window above it. In earlier times the window, which was the only one in the house, would have been covered with dried animal intestines. In 1963 it was covered with plastic that had been cut from what, in northern jargon, were euphemistically called "honey bags"; in fact they were disposable toilet receptacles used in Euro-Canadian homes in the settlement. These provided, then, the only source of exterior light in the houses. (I had had difficulty sleeping in the white tents in the summer camps, with the twenty-four hours of sunlight that flooded the high Arctic in mid-summer, but had no trouble in the dark interiors of the houses of Aullativik.) The walls were papered over with old newspapers and magazines found in garbage bags in the settlement.

The buildings themselves were constructed of sod and scrap lumber, and covered with the summer tent, or *tupic*. Within a month or so after they had been occupied, camp houses began to accumulate a cover of drifting snow, and before winter had progressed far they were protected by several feet of white insulation. Dogs would then move from the front of the houses to the roofs to soak up conducted heat, and the interiors would reverberate as animals joined nightly in a discordant chorus of howling. Tununermiut dogs could not bark, a genetic reflection, I assumed, of wolf ancestry.

In time, when snow conditions were right for the construction of houses, round entry halls made of snow blocks were built on to the fronts of houses. These were used to store meat and hunting equipment such as rifles. In front of the central house in Aullativik that year a storage unit was built to be used by all households in the camp. This open-topped snow-block structure was used to store meat and fish, and was the only one of its kind that I saw in any of the camps.

I gained some small personal insight into the realities of a subsistence economy when a young dog that I had befriended developed distemper during the winter and had to be shot. His body was placed on a rim of the ice house, and there it remained in full public view until some months later, when one of the women decided to skin it and use the hair for parka trim. The idea that it had been a pet to me, and that I might be somewhat sentimental about it, was highly alien to the people. On the other hand, they saw in the corpse a practical use of which I had not been aware.

The Tununermiut houses did not have the high sleeping platforms found among some other Inuit, but there were raised areas in them. Inside each house was a kind of cut-out effect, with slightly raised wooden platforms on either side and an elevated sleeping platform across the rear. On a normal day, if hunting had been good, one reached the centre of the home by stepping over or around a seal carcass. In most of the houses the left side, as viewed by someone entering at the front door, was the domestic or kitchen area. This was the domain of the woman of the household. On the raised platform were found the *kudlik*, used for heating and cooking, and the woman's smoking materials, such as a can of tobacco and cigarette papers. Any other personal possessions of the woman of the house would also be kept in this area. When other women came to visit her, they would usually sit beside her on the sleeping platform.

The raised area on the right was the domain of the male of the house and his male friends. There, men would sit and discuss earlier hunts, anticipate future ones, or simply exchange gossip. Silence in social settings was not feared by the Tununermiut, and either men or women might sit together for hours, smoking and drinking tea, with never a word exchanged. As someone who had been socialized in a much more frantic social milieu, I needed time to learn to be comfortable in visiting an Inuit home and sharing a cup of tea, then leaving having exchanged only a cursory greeting with my host. In time, I learned to value this very sane use of silence.

The male side of the house was where the husband would repair his hunting and fishing equipment, and carve, if he had the talent. (The Tununermiut men of that period knew that there was always a market for their soapstone carvings, but men carved only when hunting had been poor and they needed cash to purchase food or other commodities at the trading post in Pond Inlet.) At camp church services, held twice every Sunday in each camp, the separate domains of the two sexes were respected, with women sitting on the sleeping platform near the woman's side, men on their platform, and children in the middle.

The basic house plan I have described was found in all five of the Aullativik houses when we moved into them in early fall 1963. During the winter, however, Qamaniq's was strikingly changed when he built wooden beds and tables from scrap lumber found in the settlement. I was never completely clear as to why he made these changes, but I do regard them as evidence of his innovativeness and creative qualities. Later, when he and his family made the transition to sedentary life in Pond Inlet, these qualities served him well as he became a local entrepreneur. I am convinced that he was not attempting to emulate Euro-Canadian homes specifically, but instead merely saw the innovations as ways of expressing his individuality. A born leader, he took satisfaction from doing things that suggested that he marched to a different drummer.

Most Tununermiut of the early 1960s had few material possessions. (Exceptions were those who had secured wage employment with Euro-Canadian agencies in Pond Inlet.) Some of the basic items of material culture found in Aullativik homes would also have been found in pre-contact houses, such as the *kudlik*, which was the woman's responsibility, and the *ulu*, a half-moon shaped woman's knife. In some homes a harpoon might be propped up against a wall or stuck into the snow in the entry area, but in most cases they would be simple metal rods with sharpened points that had been recovered from the debris of discarded house-building materials in the settlement. All families had primus stoves, but these were, as mentioned earlier, used primarily by men on hunting trips to make tea at rest stops and in their trail snow houses.

On the other hand, in most homes a number of items of more recent vintage would be found. In Aullativik, the most valued possession of women fortunate enough to own one was a hand-operated sewing machine. The price of seal skins was artificially inflated in the early 1960s because of a southern fad for seal-skin trimmed clothing and seal-skin boots. (This was before the controversy over the hunting of baby seals caught the public attention.) At the same time, the caribou herds that roamed over northern Baffin Island, and had never been large, were diminished. Consequently, Tununermiut found it more economical to wear clothing the women made from cloth purchased at the trading post, except for seal-skin boots and caribou-hide parkas. (In fact, the majority of men did not own caribou parkas. I was unable to obtain one because hides were simply not available.) The primitive sewing machines were important, therefore, in the manufacture of clothing. Three Aullativik women owned their own machines and prized them dearly, but each was always willing to loan her machine to a neighbour or relative. Traditional patterns of sharing were extended even to these status items.

In terms of hunting technology, the Tununermiut had replaced the harpoons of their ancestors with the rifles used since the whaling period. The exception to this was a young man in another camp who was reputed to use a harpoon in hunting. He was a deviant in several respects, never having married and continuing to live well into adulthood with his parents. No one could satisfactorily explain to me his preference for a harpoon over a rifle, and my Aullativik informants thought he was foolish to do so. I speculated on whether he might be an incipient shaman, but the derision directed to him at social events he attended in the settlement suggested that he did not have the presence for that role. Very likely he was mentally retarded, but capable enough not to be a burden to other members of his camp.

In any event, rifles were the most valued possession of Tununermiut men. In Aullativik, four of the adult men had single-shot .22s, which they used to hunt small game such as rabbit and ptarmigan. Qamaniq, the incipient capitalist, had a high-powered telescopic lens on his .22, which probably contributed to his hunting success. He owned the only .222 in the camp, but others aspired to one of their own, as evidenced by the fact that when I paid Jimmy Muckpah at the end of my stay with his family, the first item he purchased was a .222. All Aullativikmiut men had World War I .303s, heavy, high-powered rifles designed to kill people. The men of the camp used them to hunt everything from ducks to polar bears. The reason was that they received free ammunition for .303s, whereas they had to buy bullets for their .22s, and that was only possible when they had skins to trade. They had been issued the .303s as members of the Canadian government's Ground Observer Corps, and as long as they remained members of the Corps they received an annual issue of ammunition. In return, they were expected to watch the Arctic skies for sightings of foreign aircraft and to report any sightings. In moments of depression my spirits soared at the sight of men, faithful to their duty, watching high-flying jets streak across the sky, then running into their houses to look up the markings in their English code books, and finally throwing up their hands and laughing. Even if they identified the markings of a low-flying aircraft, they could not afford to interrupt their hunting to take the trip to Pond Inlet to report it.

Transistor radios could be found in many Tununermiut camp houses, and there were two in Aullativik, owned by Qamaniq and Jimmy Muckpah. Qamaniq also owned a portable phonograph, which he used that winter in an ingenious manner to provide a kind of radio station for the camp. He took the detachable speaker from his phonograph and installed it in the home of his father, Arniatsiark, and then connected the turntable to his own radio. Extensions connected the turntable with the radio in Jimmy Muckpah's house and the speaker in Arniatsiark's house. When Qamaniq played his Johnny Cash recordings after that, they could be heard in three separate houses. He and the other men constructed a large antenna on the hill behind the camp and attached it to the two radios so as to improve reception.

The radios in Aullativik provided an important link with the outside world. Despite the archaic state of the two radios, Aullativik was unusually well situated for reception of radio signals. Each night we listened to a country and western station in Wheeling, West Virginia, and I received word of the assassination of John F. Kennedy from a station in Dallas, Texas, minutes after the tragedy occurred. Every Wednesday evening all Aullativikmiut in the camp that day would gather in Jimmy Muckpah's home, the largest in the camp, to listen to the half-hour Inuit-language broadcast carried on the CBC Northern Service. The announcer, Ann Padlo, was from Pond Inlet herself, and her family still lived in the settlement, so the program of information and news had special meaning for the Tununermiut. The Aullativikmiut also listened regularly to Inuit-language programs on the Godthaab (Greenland) station, which carried dramatized versions of Inuit legends and discussions of threats to the possible retention of Inuit identity and culture, which were beginning to trouble the Greenlanders. The accents of the Greenlanders were subtly ridiculed, but their discussions were taken seriously. I can recall Jimmy Muckpah expressing deep concern at hearing that use of the Inuit language was dying out in Greenland.

Every adult male had at least one *Komatik*, or sled, and most had two. In Aullativik all had two. They were the heavy *Komatiks* of the high eastern Arctic, made to be strong and sturdy, yet flexible, so that they could take the punishment meted out by winter travel in darkness over ice that had broken and refrozen at least once before hardening permanently, and so was littered with sharp outcrops. They could plunge over five-foot-high precipices without being seriously damaged. The traditional runners of whale bones had been replaced by wooden ones covered with metal strips, purchased at the Bay post. Some men would have two sleds, one small one for hunting and a heavier one for use on long trips and family visits to the settlement. Whichever one was not in use at any given time was turned upside down and placed on two gasoline drums, thus becoming a useful storage unit for food and unused equipment that would not be hurt by freezing, but had to be kept out of the reach of dogs.

There was only one kayak in Tununermiut country in 1963 — it was owned by the area administrator in Pond Inlet, who had brought it with him from Cape Dorset, his previous posting. Instead, canoes and small rowboats were used, all powered by outboard motors. In Aullativik the four male household heads all had their own boat and motors, and Qamaniq had two motors. There was also a whale-boat — a bulky, old Peterhead craft powered by an inboard engine. The boat was under the control of Arniatsiark, the headman, but was communally owned. It was used mainly for the transportation of women and children in moves between the summer and winter camps, and for occasional summer trips by families to the settlement of Pond Inlet.

Other personal possessions of Tununermiut individuals and families consisted of clothing, kerosene lamps in a few homes, the sewing tools of women, and the hunting equipment of men, such as butchering knives. Every family had a store-bought saw, used in house construction and repair and, on occasion, in place of the traditional snow knife to cut blocks of snow for trail snowhouses. Most men had a few assorted tools, which were loaned freely back and forth between them. All of the men had wrist watches, and some of the families owned alarm clocks, which were used to signal important events, such as church services, but rarely for awakening people.

Other than as a call to services, the Tununermiut of that period had little use for the clock. Children slept when they were tired and climbed from their blankets when they were refreshed or hungry. Men slept for long periods after returning from hunting trips, but on the trips used their internal biological clocks to regulate time, usually sleeping for short periods of four or five hours at a time. On such hunting trips they would keep going, often for twenty or more hours, until fatigue had reached the level at which the cold began to wear on them. Only then would they stop and build a snowhouse in which to rest. This attitude towards time was to present a problem when, a few years later, families moved to Pond Inlet, where the men found wage labour and the children began to attend school. In Aullativik they used watches and clocks to tell the hour and to some extent for planning, but they were not yet bound by their tyranny.

The introduction of personal and largely non-utilitarian items such as watches and radios seemed to me, at the time, to be having radical effects on Tununermiut conceptions of personal property. Traditionally, of course, material items had been limited to handmade tools and weapons, and hunting crafts such as kayaks and sleds. With the exceptions of such things as children's toys, virtually everything owned was utilitarian and related to subsistence activities. Wealth was not measured in terms of personal property, although an individual who was a better craftsman than his fellow band members might be envied his own equipment. It was obviously an inconvenience and a burden for highly mobile people to accumulate excessive material goods. Men did cache meat under rocks, and a good hunter might have more caches than others, but meat was not considered a personal possession, and an individual would be honour-bound to share his supply with kinspeople and other members of his band. Taking meat from another man's cache was completely appropriate behaviour if one was in need of food. This implicit and deeply engrained pattern of generosity even extended to hunting implements, which were freely shared, at times without the explicit consent of the owner.

The traditional pattern of free borrowing is illustrated in a situation that I observed in the fall of 1963. One of the RCMP special constables, a Tununermiut, was on a hunting trip in the vicinity of Aullativik and, as was customary, spent the night at the camp. He was travelling by canoe. Two days after he left, the waters of Eclipse Sound froze over. Several weeks later, the men from Aullativik went to the site of the abandoned summer camp to retrieve some household utensils that had been left there. Jimmy Muckpah also intended to bring back the second of his own sleds, which he had left nearby the previous spring. Since they had not planned to spend another winter at Aullativik, he had decided to leave the sled at a more convenient location. On our arrival we discovered that the sled was gone. The special constable had left a cache of gasoline near where the sled had been stored, and everyone assumed that he had taken it. No concern was expressed, and we returned to Aullativik. When we next visited the settlement some weeks later, Jimmy learned that the ice had formed before the special constable had left the Aullativik area, and consequently he had been unable to return home by canoe. He had taken the sled, loaded his boat and gear on it, and pulled it across Eclipse Sound to Bylot Island, a distance of at least fifty miles. He left the sled at the local camp, Illukisaat, and arranged for transportation back across to Pond Inlet. Before returning to Aullativik, we made a long detour to Bylot Island to retrieve the sled, and that was the end of the affair. I was gently ridiculed when I asked why the special constable hadn't been expected to return the sled himself.

One anecdote, of course, doesn't make a generalization, but shortly before my departure in 1964 I administered a questionnaire to all adult Tununermiut, which had been designed to explore the ways in which individuals and categories of individuals (such as males and females), interpreted Canadian law and governmental processes and structures. Part of it consisted of a series of hypothetical situations in which an individual was confronted with a choice between resolving a problem by observing Canadian law, or resorting to traditional Inuit legal norms. One of these raised the question of what a person would do if someone had raided his meat cache without asking his permission, and all respondents answered that if such a situation did occur, the person would obviously have been in need of the food, and no reprisal would be sought.

To return to my point, however, such recent acquisitions as watches and radios, although of recognized utility, were not directly related to subsistence activities, and I thought that I saw emerging trends in their use that would alter drastically the traditional pattern of free borrowing. For example, a rifle or harpoon might be loaned out for a few days while the owner remained in camp, say, repairing other equipment, but a radio would be used daily by his wife or him as long as one of them was in camp, and taken along on forays into the interior in search of caribou. I will say more on this topic in a later chapter, but as things turned out, my prediction of an emerging acquisitive ethic was basically incorrect. In 1973, when I returned to Pond Inlet, although the material possessions found in Tununermiut homes had increased immensely as a consequence of full-time involvement in a wage economy, permanent residence, enlarged homes, and a sharply increased level of affluence among virtually everyone, traditional patterns of free borrowing were still maintained and in some ways had become a mechanism for the retention of Inuit identity.

Contact-Traditional Economics

Soapstone carving had become a basic industry in many Canadian Inuit communities by 1963, but little carving was done by the Tununermiut. Each month a few pieces would turn up in the HBC post in Pond Inlet, to be either placed on display for possible purchase by an occasional pilot or other visitor to the settlement, or shipped south to Winnipeg for distribution to southern Canadian outlets, but in general the Tununermiut resisted the idea of regular carving. Jimmy Muckpah made several pieces for me, as a personal favour, but he and Kadloo were the only Aullativikmiut to carve, and Jimmy found it a tedious activity, not fully worthy of a hunter. When he did carve, he would joke about his need for "cold cash." As full-time hunters, the men of Aullativik provided the food staples for their families, and their hunting activities enabled them to trade seal skins for other foodstuffs such as flour, tea, sugar, and salt. Only emergencies would induce men to turn to carving.

Meat was the main staple, and the basic meat was seal, which was hunted year round, by boat in summer and on and through ice in winter. There is an average of two months of open water each year on Eclipse Sound and Navy Board Inlet, and men would begin to use their boats as soon as the first cracks appeared in the ice. Conversely, sleds were put to use in early fall before the ice had even hardened. I can recall sitting on a sled going across newly formed ice with the sled creating an effect like that of a finger being traced across the top of a freshly baked sponge cake; a few days later, I ran alongside a sled that left behind it a channel of thin fractured ice. To stop on either occasion, even momentarily, would have been disastrous. But the men were excited about getting their sleds out.

In fall, when ice formed, boats and canoes were strapped on top of sleds and taken to the increasingly distant last remnants of open water for the final summer hunting of the year. In winter, breathing-hole hunting was still practised. It is possibly the most punishing form of hunting known, for the hunter had to stand motionless for perhaps several hours over a breathing hole, waiting for the sounds of a seal taking in air. (The Tununermiut had given up much of the technology traditionally used in breathing-hole hunting, such as down indicators, if in fact they had ever used them. This equipment is effectively demonstrated in some of the Netsilik films made by Asen Balicki, with which some readers may be familiar.)

By 1963 the traditional back-breaking and bone-chilling technique had been supplemented by the use of seal nets. Artificial breathing holes were made a few yards across the ice from an actively used one, and nets strung between them beneath the ice. The nets had to be examined almost daily, for otherwise sea lice would attack the skins of trapped animals, making them unmarketable and of no use for clothing. One incident that I observed in 1963 illustrated the importance of cooperation even in such an individualistic society as that of the Tununermiut. On this occasion, two of the men from Aullativik and I had gone on an extended hunting trip, leaving the nets in the care of another individual who had elected to hunt in the vicinity of the camp. We returned several days later to find the holes so frozen over that it took hours to break them free, and the nets were badly damaged as a consequence. The two hunters were furious, and seriously considered demanding that the individual responsible leave the camp permanently. Eventually they decided that he could remain, but with a harsh reprimand as punishment. His explanation was that during our absence he had decided on the spur of the moment to take his family on a trip to another camp. He was the least competent hunter in the camp, and had a weak power base, so the threatened banishment might well have been carried out. However, it was his very incompetence that probably saved him, for the other men laughed at their own foolishness in having left him with more responsibility than he could handle.

During the winter of 1963 in Aullativik the seal nets yielded, on the average, approximately two seals per week for each household. This was barely enough food for the dogs, but it did provide skins for trading. Breathing-hole hunting brought even lower returns, and so the people were heavily dependent upon meat that had been cached the previous spring and summer. As the caches were depleted and hunting became less productive during the later months of winter, there were several periods when there was no meat in the camp. During these, the children would become drawn and thin as they subsisted on bannock, if indeed flour was available. On one occasion we "raided" a cache of a narwhal left by a marine biologist the previous summer. He had told the local people to leave the meat, as it was full of parasites, but that did not bother them. I recall their laughter when the men uncovered the rancid meat and cut off large pieces of skin to eat on the spot. They thought that this was one meat that I would not share with them, but even though my hunger pangs had diminished after days without food, I forced myself to join them, and in the act passed through one more informal rite of passage.

The reawakening of the land that comes with the arrival of spring is possibly more breath-taking in the mountainous regions surrounding Pond Inlet than in any other part of the Canadian Arctic. The sun begins to cast its reflection on the taller cliffs in late February or early March, and by April it has returned in its full glory, shining brilliantly for close to twenty-four hours each day, and heralding the return of the female seals and their cubs. In late spring hunting was at its best; the young seals and their mothers would climb out onto the ice to sun themselves, thus becoming easy prey for hunters, who would creep close to them while hidden behind white screen-covered props. During this period men would often move their families from their own winter camps to others where the hunting might be better, and some camps would swell with newcomers while others would be virtually abandoned. As the ever-present sun melted the upper layers of ice, however, and the first cracks appeared in the ice, the old groups would reform and move to their summer camps, usually in late May or early June.

The staple of Tununermiut diet during the contact-traditional period, then, was seal, and most of the hunters' time was spent in quest of it. However, from late spring to early fall caribou herds roamed the interior of Baffin Island, and although the herds had been diminished, families eagerly looked forward to forays inland in search of them. During the summer months, the arctic goose and several varieties of duck were hunted, and ptarmigan and arctic hare sporadically throughout fall and winter. In summer, during periods of open water, arctic char was fished with nets, and during early fall men would fish the inland lakes through newly formed ice. The fish was usually stored in caches and used during the winter for dog food and as a supplement to the human diet. Bannock and tea rounded out the diet, although handfuls of dried vegetables and, in particular, dried onions were often tossed into soups and stews. Small amounts of canned food were purchased in Pond Inlet, but they were generally used up before the men had been back in camp for two or three days. When it was available in the HBC store, candy was always bought for the children when the men were in to trade — the beginning of an ominous trend in nutrition and dental health.

Women would visit the settlement at festive times such as Christmas and usually two or three times each summer, but in general the men of Aullativik made the food purchases, and consequently had considerable control over dietary patterns. Women would make suggestions, but what was purchased largely depended on what was available, and so men exercised a great deal of individual choice in the matter. In some camps, located nearer to the settlement, women more often accompanied men on trips in to trade skins, and so this domestic pattern was not invariant. The Aullativikmiut visited the settlement at least once every six weeks, and usually once each month, and they would normally return home one day after arrival, unless the trip coincided with a weekend, in which case they would remain for the church service at the Anglican mission on Sunday. As a rule, two or three men would make the trip together, often sharing one canoe or boat on summer trips.

Sexual Roles and Division of Labour

Some years ago I heard a paper, delivered at an anthropological

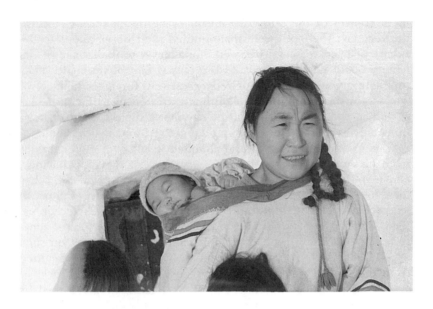

Elisapee and Suzy Muckpah. Aullativik, 1963.

conference, in which Inuit men were characterized as hulking, demanding male chauvinists and their wives as poor, desperate crea-
tures who spent their days huddled over a *kudlik*. As Jean Briggs
(1974) has vividly described elsewhere, such a characterization is a
caricature, entirely unfair to Inuit women and their contemporary
role in settlements such as Pond Inlet, where women hold several
prominent and powerful elective offices in the formal political
structures. It also conveys a false image of Inuit males.

As the discussion of food-purchasing patterns suggests, the division of economic and other activities between males and females
in contact-traditional Tununermiut society was too complex and
interconnected to be dismissed by rhetoric, however well-inten-
tioned. The person who delivered the paper I heard had been influenced by the available literature on the Inuit, from which it is
not difficult to extract an image of chauvinistic male hunters domi-
nating their women and trading them back and forth as if they
were property. This conception can, I believe, be explained in two
ways. In the first place, with a few notable exceptions the ethnographers of the Inuit have been male. And given that they were
willing to do field work among the Inuit in the first place, they
must have often been men of adventuresome spirit who were en-
amoured of the hunt itself, and its activities. It is possible that for

them control of the hunt also meant social dominance. Secondly, the very fact that they were male limited their observations to the sphere of male activity. They were not as privy to the female realm, and so could not describe it as they could that of the male. They probably are not to be criticized excessively for their failings, of course, for they were products of their own time and of a particular period in the history of anthropology. Nevertheless, their descriptions are, as a consequence, typically skewed and male oriented.

Being a male, I was naturally limited in my own opportunities to make consistent and regular observations of female behaviour, and I tended to act within the male sphere. Jimmy and the other men had taken me seriously when I told them that I wanted to learn to live like an Inuit, and this meant that I usually accompanied them on hunts and other travels. During this period, of semi-sedentary camp life, women only infrequently went along on such expeditions. At the same time, though, I was not totally excluded from the female sphere, at times because of simple good luck.

On three occasions while I lived at Aullativik I was forced by illness to remain in camp while the men went off on hunting trips, and on each I was able to observe Tununermiut women in the absence of their men. One special situation, which I initially regarded as a disaster, afforded me a special opportunity to observe female behaviour. I had made arrangements in the spring of 1964 to borrow a dogteam and sled from a friend in Pond Inlet and to visit Illukisaat, his father's camp on Bylot Island. I had received an invitation from the father, who was also headman in the camp, some weeks before, and I had planned to spend two weeks with his family. Apparently the father forgot about the arrangements, and I arrived to discover that the men were all away on an extended hunting trip; only women and children were left. The headman's wife, a gentle and hospitable matron, seemed undistressed by the situation and invited me to stay in her home for two weeks anyway. In spite of some reservations I accepted her kind offer, feeling that I would be discourteous to do otherwise. I was not sure what I would do with my time, feeling rather awkward, but soon realized that I had been afforded rare opportunity to observe female interaction patterns in the absence of males in a setting other than Aullativik. My presence made the situation somewhat artificial, of course, and my feelings of discomfort must have been obvious, but Inuit hospitality prevailed and I soon became as much as possible part of the scenery. Much of my time, when I was not caring for my dogs or visiting, was spent sitting on a small cliff overlooking the camp and watching the activities below. (Perhaps this is a good

Woman cleaning seal skin. Aullativik, 1963.

place to mention that during the entire time I lived with the Tununermiut I was never offered sexual hospitality, nor did I ever request it.)

Anthropologists have written extensively in recent years about patterns of bonding among males in hunting societies. Certainly, cooperation between Tununermiut men was an essential component of their relations with one another in economic and other affairs. However, the converse, female bonding, was a decided aspect of female relationships among the Tununermiut. Instead of sitting hunched over their *kudliks*, Tununermiut women spent much of their time visiting back and forth in their homes or in the open air. They would, as I've mentioned, freely borrow equipment such as sewing machines from one another, and would pass cans of tobacco back and forth when sharing a kettle of tea. I was never fluent enough in Inuktitut to be able to follow carefully their conversations with one another (for I was always in the role of eavesdropper when listening to them), but I did note that their talk was filled with humour and interspersed with a great deal of laughter. Like women in southern society, they discussed their children, plans for their next shopping trip to the settlement, and other such matters. There was much joking about their husbands and other men, with explicit sexual references. While the woman who was hostess would work away on a parka she was making for her husband or a child, or a new pair of boots, her visitor would sit beside her on the sleeping platform smoking and making suggestions. It was not so much an economic bonding, then, for each woman was highly independent in fulfilling her own domestic obligations, but rather one of social and psychological sharing.

To return to the topic of the division of labour between males and females, it has to be admitted that in both traditional and contact-traditional Tununermiut the men were the hunters, and hunting skills were both highly valued and the basis for the acquisition of overt political authority and influence. However, once an animal had been killed and skinned, the processing of the hide and carcass usually became the responsibility of the wife. If the animal was to be cached, it would be buried "on the trail" by the hunter, after the skin had been cut off. If it was brought back to the camp, the hunter would skin it and then cut away the thick fatty tissue just under the skin, which the wife would then render into fat for cooking and heating. (A popular image of the Inuit at table is of individuals consuming large hunks of raw blubber. Contrary to this stereotype, although the Tununermiut of the contact-traditional period did favour fatty meat, seal was the main staple in their larders, and once the outer layer of fat has been removed from a seal the meat that is left is not fatty or even marbled. It is somewhat oily, however, and has a rich, sweet taste. Seal meat is an acquired taste for the southerner, but after existing on it for several months I found that I preferred it to beef. Because of its odor, many southern visitors to the Arctic disdain to eat it, and thereby forgo a special culinary experience. They often limit themselves to the liver and heart, which are less aromatic and oily.)

Lard purchased at the HBC post would be used for frying, if it was available, but the men preferred their bannock made with seal oil. Bannock made this way would not freeze, and so chunks could be broken off a loaf and eaten with a mug of tea at rest breaks when on the trail. Seal oil was a staple of the diet.

The women would then scrape the skin clean of any residue of fat, wash it, and string it on a drying rack. Once it was dried, the women would scrape off the oily residue from the underside, roll up the skin, and store it in the tent or house until it was time to trade it or make it into a pair of boots, or possibly cut it in a circular, coil-like manner to fashion a long bullwhip.

The feeding of the ever-hungry dogs was a procedure in itself, carried out jointly by men and women. The men would cut the meat into small pieces and feed the pups and nursing bitches first, while the women stood about them in a circle wielding whips and staves to ward off the howling males. If meat was meant for human consumption, it would be cut up by the women outdoors in the summer, or, in colder times of the year, the carcass would be brought into the house to be taken apart meal by meal.

Like other Inuit, the Tununermiut had traditionally eaten most of their meat raw, but by 1963–64 they increasingly cooked their food. Meat, if cooked, was either fried or boiled. Frying was done over a primus stove and was usually limited to the heart and liver.

Normally only one main meal was eaten each day, and if no one felt like cooking even this was omitted. Children and adults alike ate whenever they felt like it, if food was available, and children could often be seen walking from house to house chewing on a piece of leathery meat. When meals were prepared, bannock was always a part of them, and was at other times used as a filler when there was no meat. On special occasions, or when the wife of the house felt the urge to make them, pancakes were prepared, and if enough money had been left over after basic foodstuffs were purchased at the store, coffee boiled in a pot would be served with the pancakes. Women always made the bannock and pancakes in camps, but on the trail men would, of course, do their own cooking, which was usually limited to frying liver. (I was never certain whether meat was cooked on hunting trips in deference to my own preference for cooked meat or because it was their practice. I regularly ate raw meat in the camp, and even developed a taste for raw seal and caribou meat and fish.) The men ate camp-cooked meals about one-third of the time.

The stereotyped image of the Inuit woman had some basis in fact, in that women did spend much of their time sitting on their side of the sleeping platform. However, there was always a backlog of tasks to be performed while sitting, and there was usually a companion to help pass the time. Some of these tasks were from a southern perspective onerous, such as chewing seal-skin boots. If these become wet, they dry into a cardboard-like state. If they are not too stiff, they can be softened by walking in them through soft snow, but if they are too hard to be forced onto the feet they must be chewed, and it was the chore of the women to soften them in this way.

On the other hand, of course, the Tununermiut women were not forced to go on the long, punishing hunting trips, during which men would often travel for hours at a time in bone-chilling temperatures, stopping for a few hours of sleep in a hastily built snowhouse and then venturing on once again. Women did not have to pull seal nets from the water, feeling them freeze almost instantly in the Arctic air. There was excitement in the hunts, and men looked forward to them, but they were not easy, and women in contact-traditional periods were spared them. When the men were out, women would visit back and forth and houses would resound with laughter at the stories told, but there was also an underlying tension, a fear that the men would return from the hunt without meat, or perhaps not return at all. The stress of these circumstances was greater for women than for men, I believe, for men were to some extent in control of the hunting, and thus the food supply, while the women had to stay behind and worry. The female social bonding described earlier was very likely in large part an adaptive technique for dissipating the anxiety produced by this stress. Laughter is commonly used in human societies to mask and relieve psychological tension, and the joking between women when men were out on a hunt served this function. Men, of course, also suffered from the anxiety of not knowing if they would be successful, and much laughter and joking occurred among them while hunting.

When men returned from a hunt either with freshly killed animals or meat from caches, they would stop a mile or so out on the ice, in view of the twinkling lights of the camp in the distance, chop the frozen meat into small pieces, and then unharness and feed their dogs. This was done to ensure that their own dogs, weary from the trip, would be fed before the other camp dogs. There was, then, a pragmatic reason for the pause, but it also had overtones of sexual posturing, for after having eaten, the dogs would be driven into a frenzy by the whips and shouts of the men, and would streak across the ice to cover the last distance home. Women and children, alerted by the cries of the dogs, would toss jackets over their shoulders and run out to meet the approaching teams and assist in the unharnessing.

No matter what the time of night or day, families would then retire to their own homes and husbands and wives would sit up for hours recounting the events of the hunting trip and gossiping about what had happened in the camp while the men had been away.

Care and Training of the Young

Like food preparation, child training among the Tununermiut in 1963 was a joint venture of husband and wife. The "favorite son" complex was very much a part of Tununermiut domestic life, with the status usually conferred on the youngest male child. This child received preferential treatment at the hands of his parents, and it was an act of foolhardiness for an older sibling to mistreat his or her youngest brother, even if, until the latest birth in the family, that sibling had been the favourite son himself. Until a child was weaned, it was the exclusive concern of the mother, who would fuss over it and in general behave in a highly indulgent manner. To a lesser extent the child would be coddled by the father and other siblings. As it matured, it would increasingly become the responsibility of an older sister or female cousin, even if that person was only eight or nine years old. A woman's parka would usually be made for the sister/cousin, and she would carry her young ward about the camp on her back in the outer hood while she played with her peers. In this way the mother was free to either indulge a new infant if there was one or to engage in other activities that she considered important. She would be constantly on the watch for times when the older daughter might be less permissive with the child in her care than tradition allowed. As a rule, the world of children in contact-traditional Tununermiut homes, once they had passed infancy, was in many respects separate from that of adults. Particularly in summer, children would play at any and all hours of the day or night. I remember often waking on mornings to find small children coming home to sleep after a night of activity (the midnight sun gave them light during summer nights).

When boys reached the age of about ten years, they quickly lost any favourite status they may have enjoyed and began training for adulthood. At that age they began to be taken along with the men on short hunting trips, or to check on the seal nets or the fox line. From then on they left behind the protected world of the home and increasingly were given new responsibilities. In spring, for example, a young man might be taken along with his older, married brother on a hunting trip, and told to control the dogs while the brother crept up on a seal basking in the sun. Responsibility training was standard procedure for adolescents, and youths who were negligent were subjected to the harsh verbal ridicule of fathers, brothers, and other men. I observed several adolescents in a number of camps being put through this training, but in Aullativik in 1963 only Paneelook, ten years old at the time, experienced this discontinuity in the behaviour expected of him. Until that year he had been the favoured son of his father's earlier marriage. His older brother, Qamaniq, and his brother-in-law, Jimmy Muckpah, became both his tormentors and tutors. The father, Arniatsiark, was a solitary individual who usually hunted alone, and Qamaniq was in line to replace him as headman. The two men teased the

Noah Muckpah and friends. Aullativik, 1963.

youth without mercy, but also taught him the skills of a hunter. He accepted the discontinuity joyously, for he was entering the sphere of adults: the new status he was moving towards more than compensated for the new responsibilities placed upon him. The following year Paneelook became a pupil in the new school in Pond Inlet and lost something that at the time I thought he would never recover – the pride associated with becoming a hunter. By the time I returned to Pond Inlet a decade later he had become an oil rigger, working on rigs in the high Arctic northern islands, and while I was in the field that time he submitted an application with the local Adult Education Officer to be sent south to receive training as a heavy equipment operator, as his older brother Qamaniq had done. But when he was home on periods of "rest and recuperation" he would pack his gear and go off on his own hunting trips. The skills learned in his adolescence had stayed with him, but had not been learned by his younger contemporaries.

Young girls usually had warm relationships with their fathers, but their training in adult social roles was left to their grandmothers, older sisters, and, to a lesser extent, it seemed to me, their mothers. Although they were given responsibility training at a considerably earlier age than their brothers, and from the age of five or six years would be expected to assist in caring for their younger siblings, nieces, and nephews, full adult status did not come until they married. In the contact-traditional period, that usually took place in middle to late teens.

There was one marriage among the Tununermiut during my first time with them. A sixteen-year-old girl in Aullativik, the daughter of Arniatsiark, had been betrothed in infancy to a male infant in a camp at the other side of Pond Inlet. Because of the distance between the two camps her fiancé had no opportunity to court her, and indeed, as the time for the impending marriage approached, the two young people were still virtually strangers to one another. Traditionally, the marriage would have been finalized by the two simply beginning to live with one another, either temporarily in one of the parental homes or in a residence of their own. As Canadian citizens, however, they would have to have their marriage notarized by the local police. All arrangements had been made, and the RCMP corporal in Pond Inlet was prepared to have them sign the marriage certificate.

A figurative wrench was thrown into the plans when Qamaniq, older brother of the bridegroom, went into Pond Inlet to inform the corporal that his sister did not want the marriage, and that in his opinion she was too young to be married in any event. Concerned by this, the corporal invited the two prospective marriage partners to a meeting with their parents and himself. At the meeting he asked the two if they really wanted to be married to one another, and they answered in the affirmative. He felt he had no recourse other than to perform the civil ceremony and have them sign the certificate, which they did. Aircraft only visited Pond Inlet every three months or so in the early 1960s, but one did arrive shortly after the ceremony, and the certificate was sent south on it. A few weeks later the bride, on a trip to the settlement, approached the RCMP corporal in a state of abject depression to ask that the marriage be annulled. She was informed that it had been duly registered in Ottawa, and that nothing could be done other than to file divorce proceedings. I cite this story at length because it illustrates one of the many areas of conflict between traditional customs and the imposed laws and norms of southern Canadian society. The corporal had simply done his job, which was to perform the ceremony and register the marriage certificate. He had tried to ascertain the wishes of the young Inuit couple, but had either forgotten or been ignorant of the fact that, until marriage at least, Inuit youths were respectful of their parents and their wishes, and so the couple had no choice but to acquiesce at the meeting he had arranged.

Qamaniq performed his traditional role as a brother by intervening, for older brothers in traditional Tununermiut society felt a moral responsibility for the welfare of their married and unmarried sisters. It would have been appropriate for him to have taken his sister back when he discovered that she was unhappy with her marriage, but he was too much intimidated by the potential force of Canadian law to do so.

Customary adoptions were still common among the Tununermiut during that period. In Aullativik, Jimmy Muckpah's aged mother, Attagootung, lived with her adopted daughter, who helped care for her needs, and Jimmy and his wife adopted an infant daughter while I was living with them. Jimmy was an excellent hunter and so a good provider, while the biological parents of the adopted child had more children than they could easily support. Arrangements for the adoption had been made during the pregnancy. I knew that Jimmy and his wife had lost a child the year or so before. It was killed by dogs, and I was told that because of the tragic event the wife, Elisapee, did not want any more children of her own. Speaking of the need to adopt, she explained that she was temporarily infertile. It is possible that the psychological trauma associated with the loss of the child had an effect on her ability to conceive, but in any event, although she did not want to give birth again, she did want a baby, and so the adoption had been arranged with the full consent of both families.

We had gone to Pond Inlet for the Christmas and New Year's festivities, and on our return made a detour to the camp of the biological parents to retrieve the two-week-old girl, Suzy. It was a bitterly cold day, and I recall vividly the long trip back to Aullativik with the baby and adoptive mother huddled on a sled under several layers of caribou hides. I feared for their well-being, and for that of the two older children, because I had been taught by Jimmy that the only way to keep from freezing one's limbs on a long dogteam trip was to run alongside the sled as much as possible. When we stopped a few miles from Aullativik while the men recovered meat from a cache, I took the boy, Noah, the mother, and the infant on one sled and drove the dogs as vigorously as I could in order to get to the camp before they froze to death. I was probably worried unduly, for no one seemed as concerned. (This was only one of several occasions when my inexperience caused me to worry about potential tragedies that did not create any anxiety in my Inuit companions.) The infant and the older children all survived the trip, and little Suzy soon became the centre of attraction in Jimmy and Elisapee's household.

Although Suzy was a girl, she had been greatly desired by her adoptive parents, and I found it intriguing to see that she usurped the favoured position in the family from young Noah. Noah had been given free rein in the household, even to the extent of terrorizing his sister, who was two years older than him and had had to defer to all of his demands. He surprised me even further by accepting this displacement with considerable equanimity. Both he and his seven-year-old sister lavished affection and attention on their new sister, and I saw no evidence of sibling rivalry on the part of either.

When they could, pregnant women would travel to Pond Inlet to give birth, but it wasn't always possible to do so. The small nursing station in the settlement was sanitary and comfortable but there was no nurse in residence, and so Inuit midwives performed the necessary obstetric operations or, in cases of possible complications, they were performed by the RCMP corporal. In serious emergencies, weather conditions permitting, women would be evacuated by aircraft to Frobisher Bay. It was not always possible, of course, to make the trip even to Pond Inlet from a distant camp. On November 11, 1963, a sled was driven onto the shoreline in front of Aullativik and disgorged a young woman bundled tightly against the wind and cold. She was taken into the house of her mother, Attagootung, and soon all of the women in the camp had joined her. The house was small, measuring less than thirty cubic feet of floor space, but they all managed to get in. The father, Pauloosie, who was the son of a camp headman and the nephew of Arniatsiark, joined his brother-in-law, Jimmy Muckpah, at the latter's home, where they were soon joined by the other men. While the women kept vigil through the night, the men played cards, joked, and also stayed awake. Before morning a son had been born, and an air of great jubilation pervaded the camp.

The roles of men and women among the Tununermiut were, then, complementary. Women were not docile, and I can remember at least one occasion when a wife struck her husband on the face for an alleged indiscretion, and many when husbands were severely cowed by their wives' sharp verbal attacks. If all did not go well for a Tununermiut wife, everyone else in her camp soon knew about it.

Hunting Patterns and Territoriality

In spite of the complementarity of their roles, during the contact-traditional period men and women did carry on their economics-related activities relatively independently of one another. In part, this was because women usually remained in the camps while men went off hunting on their own. Each camp in the Pond Inlet area was surrounded by a roughly defined territory in which men from that camp would do most of their hunting. However, it was not uncommon to encounter men from another camp, or from the settlement, hunting in one's own area. In such circumstances the two parties would sit down and share a pot of tea, trade local gossip, and then go their own ways. Strict adherence to territorial rights was not a feature of Tununermiut legal norms, at least with regard to fellow Tununermiut.

The same pattern prevailed for intra-camp hunting territories. If the men from a particular camp tended to hunt separately from one another and always followed the same routes, it was because of personal preference. In Aullativik, for example, the camp head-man, Arniatsiark, generally hunted alone on one side of Curry Island. The three younger men usually hunted on the other side and often hunted together, although they would also go off on forays on their own. Jimmy Muckpah and Qamaniq almost always hunted and fished together during the year I lived with them. This was in part because of their kinship ties, as Jimmy was married to Qamaniq's sister, but more importantly, I think, because of their exceptional skill as hunters.

After his child was born, Pauloosie lived in Aullativik with his mother-in-law for approximately five months before returning to his father's camp, and he would often hunt with Jimmy and Qamaniq, but he was not an efficient hunter himself. He was probably taken along because of the needed support he would receive from the other two men. On one occasion, for example, when several of us were travelling together on an extended hunting trip, he became lost, and the men erected a temporary shelter and spent hours searching and waiting for him. He eventually turned up and explained that he had taken the wrong turn — it happened in the middle of a blizzard, or what is called a "white-out" — and so had to follow the shoreline to come out in a circle. This had added several miles to his trip.

Kadloo, the fifth adult male, occasionally hunted with Jimmy and Qamaniq but more commonly on his own. He was not as effective a hunter as either of the other two and was not closely linked with either by ties of kinship. Also, that year was his first at Aullativik: the previous one had been spent at Igloolik, the home of his wife.

In each camp there was at least one male who wielded more authority than others; the headman. In one camp in 1963 there were two headmen, but this was an instance of an older man retaining his prestige although he had been replaced by a younger, more vigorous man. In one camp, Ippiarjuk, the headman was also an *angakok*, or shaman. These roles were not normally carried out by one individual, but in this case the individual was a person of immense power and authority who was feared and respected by all other Tununermiut. His camp was small, consisting only of his close kinspeople.

Camp headmen were generally middle-aged men who had acquired prestige for their hunting skills and decision-making abilities. They had no ultimate control over their fellows, as anyone was at any time free to pack up and move to another camp, but they could be highly autocratic and get away with it if their prestige remained high enough. Arniatsiark was a mild-mannered man who rarely told the others how to conduct their affairs. But one of his predecessors had been a dominant force in the camp: this was the famous Idlouk, with whom the Arctic photographer and writer Doug Wilkinson lived while gathering material for his book *Land of the Long Day*. Before moving to Resolute Bay in the late 1950s, Idlouk had governed Aullativik in a way that in 1963 was recalled with respect but little fondness.

Possibly because of his own gentle nature, Arniatsiark left much of the control of camp events and activities in the hands of Qamaniq. It was often Qamaniq who determined when men would hunt, and, to some extent, where. On hunting trips with other men, Qamaniq would decide when they would stop for the night, whether seals killed would be taken back to the camp or cached, and so on. When his temper flared, which was not an uncommon occurrence, the other men would quietly accept his rebukes. A year or so before I arrived, Jimmy Muckpah had been offered and had accepted a job as assistant clerk with the HBC store in Pond Inlet. A short time after he began his new duties Qamaniq came into the settlement to insist that he return to Aullativik, and Jimmy quickly resigned.

However, Arniatsiark, despite his mild temperament, did require observance of matters that he considered to be of critical importance. Most of these fell within the realm of religion. Shamanism was still practiced by the Tununermiut, and it was generally believed that the shaman of Ippiarjuk, to whom I referred earlier, could speak with polar bears and, sitting in his own house, watch activities in other camps; the Tununermiut were also practising Anglicans. (The Roman Catholic church had not been successful in its long-range proselytizing activities among the Tununermiut, despite its early success. There was one Catholic family in the region in 1963.) By 1963 the role of the headman as religious leader had had a major impact on both the headman's status and the behaviour of Tununermiut on Sundays. Services were held each Sunday morning in the largest house in each camp (in Aullativik, Jimmy Muckpah's), and everyone was expected to be present. I remember one occasion on which Jimmy, Qamaniq, and I returned from a hunting trip early Sunday morning in a state of exhaustion. Jimmy and I were shaken awake later, a bare two hours after falling asleep to make room on the sleeping platform for the women and children in the congregation. Qamaniq was not as unfortunate and slept late, but his father's sharp rebuke later that day ensured that he did not miss a service for the next several months. On another occasion, when we were desperately short of food, I considered shooting a seal that had reached its head above water for a breath of air on a Sunday morning, and was promptly told that if I did Arniatsiark would make me leave the camp and return to Pond Inlet. Religion was a matter of central importance to the Tununermiut, and even the shaman was a devout member of the Anglican communion. Sunday services were even held on hunting trips and hunting was eschewed for the day. (On one such trip, the men and I were playing cards one evening in a snowhouse and discovered that no one, including myself, had a pen or pencil to mark down scores. We resolved the problem by using the numbered pages of the hymnals that all carried: after each hand we would lay the books down upside down at the page corresponding to our score.)

Contact with the Settlement

Until now, I have described camp life among the Tununermiut in 1963 almost as if camps existed in a vacuum, and have underplayed the links between camps and the settlement, which was in turn the link with the outside world, or the south. I did so because during the contact-traditional period a life-style emerged that emphasized "life on the land"; despite links with the outside world, and considerable dependence upon it, that life-style was in many ways self-contained. In addition, during that period several prominent individuals living in camps made conscious attempts to both disguise the vitality of camp culture and create mechanisms for its preservation. I will return to this theme later, but for the time being will illustrate some of the links between camp and settlement.

Trips by the men of Aullativik to Pond Inlet to trade were usually made once each month, but were less regular during the winter months because fewer seal skins were then available for trading and travel was faster by power-driven canoes than by sled. Also, gasoline was needed to run the outboard motors, and without large storage facilities, camp people had to replenish their supplies regularly. For all these reasons, trade goods such as flour, tea, and sugar were much more prevalent in the camps in summer months.

In 1963 — in sharp contrast to ten years later — although the Tununermiut had been involved in a cash economy for decades, few had had opportunities to learn to handle or save money. Until fairly recently, the Hudson's Bay Company had used its own form of coinage; when a man came in to trade, the clerk would examine his skins, decide their market value, and then lay on the counter a number of these tokens. As the Inuit requested commodities, the clerk would take coins away, until all were gone and the trading for the month was completed. (If a small excess amount was left after basics had been purchased, it would be used to buy candy or toys for the children or a trinket for his wife.) By 1963 each adult male had his own account with the HBC store, but in most cases the same practice was continued, not because the resident trader encouraged it so much as because it had become institutionalized.

With the exception of those few individuals who had regular incomes via full-time employment with Euro-Canadian agencies in the settlement, then, most Tununermiut did not build up cash reserves in their accounts, and saving was virtually unknown. As a result, of course, during the poor hunting of the winter months credit would have to be extended regularly, to be repaid from the spring bounty.

Most trading was done with seal skins, although during fall and winter traplines for fox were maintained and were checked every week or so. During 1963–64, however, the price of seal skins escalated, and it was also an unproductive year for fox, so at least among the Aullativikmiut little attention was given to maintaining the traplines.

While in the settlement to trade, men would normally stay with friends or kinsmen. The homes of the Inuit clerk at the HBC store and the Inuit maintenance man and general jack-of-all-trades with the DNANR were constantly crowded with visiting camp people, whether related to them or not. Both men had large incomes relative to other Tununermiut, and larger houses than the other Inuit in the settlement who had jobs with Euro-Canadian agencies. However, being excluded from the Euro-Canadian social world, they continued their close relations with camp people and, as a consequence, were better able to maintain their Inuit identity. Both were in positions where they could systematically observe the behaviour of the Euro-Canadians in the settlement, and gained social dividends by transmitting gossip about them to visitors. A tradition that went back to the days of Sergeant Joy was that the men from the camps would always visit the RCMP office while in the settlement. These encounters allowed the RCMP officers who spoke Inuktitut to assemble information about activities in the camps, and in return they would often freely gossip with their visitors about recent developments in the settlement and the idiosyncracies of their fellow Euro-Canadians.

At Christmas most of the Tununermiut camps would be deserted while their inhabitants visited the settlement for the festivities that accompanied the season. Several church services were held, with attendances that threatened to burst the walls of the Anglican mission. It was a tradition that the HBC manager and the resident RCMP officers held a Christmas party, at which children would scramble across the floor in competition with each other for hard candies tossed in the air in huge handfuls. A dance was also a tradition, and the night was made short with the foot-stamping Scottish dances in which men and women circled the floor clasping and unclasping one another's hands. The early dances during the 1963 event were kept going for as long as an hour at a time, and after two or three of these the Euro-Canadian participants would succumb to fatigue and retire from the room. When they had all left, the individual dances would be shortened, greater variation in steps introduced, and the record player kept at work until dawn.

A large influx of camp people also took place each spring, when a form of local "northern games" was held in the settlement under the sponsorship of the HBC and the RCMP. During this period traditional games of physical skill such as tug-of-wars were held on the ice in front of the settlement. The games became a basis for dissension among the Euro-Canadians in 1963, because the teachers of the new DNANR day school thought the event should be sponsored by them and should be run as the sort of track-and-field day so commonly held in southern schools near the end of each academic year. Eventually the parties agreed that the games would be co-sponsored, but the debate contributed to a bruised state of inter-agency relationships.

The camps would again be virtually abandoned in middle or

late August for the annual sealift. Most of the HBC store supplies for the coming year and provisions for private members of other Euro-Canadian agencies were brought north on the *C.D. Howe*, a combined supply ship and floating hospital. Almost every able-bodied man in the area would be hired to unload the ship, a task that would last day and night for three or four days. Tents would be put up on the beach in front of and on both sides of the settlement, and while the men and older boys unloaded, their wives would visit with one another, renewing contact with friends and relatives whom they might not have seen for several months or even for the past year. If the ship arrived before the main influx of people into the settlement, its helicopter would visit the nearby camps and bring in residents for dental attention, x-rays, and other medical examinations. The men were apparently well paid for their work, but payment was in the form of credit with the HBC store rather than in cash. Shortly after completion of the sealift families would begin to move back to their summer camps, or, if it was late enough in the season, to their winter camps. The RCMP officer exerted pressure on stragglers to return to the camps as soon as possible. (In the summer of 1963 a number of families remained in the settlement for several weeks after sealift; eventually the men were called to a meeting at which they were urged to go back to hunting to ensure that they would have enough dogfood to get them through the winter months.)

During 1963–64 a considerable amount of construction went on in the settlement – primarily by DNANR, which was building a new school and two student hostels as well as more housing for personnel. Several young men were employed on this construction, although usually only temporarily; they returned to the land after a few months.

In 1963–64 all of the men from Aullativik worked for varying periods of time at an iron mine that was being developed at Mary River, located approximately one hundred miles from Aullativik. Three men were taken out by company aircraft in August to assist in the unloading of a cargo ship, and remained at the mine for approximately ten days. Apparently they were paid high wages for their work, but again in the form of credit at the HBC store in Pond Inlet. None of the men were certain of how much they had earned or if they had been paid by the day or the hour. The following spring Jimmy Muckpah was taken to the mine to work as an unskilled labourer and receive training as a heavy equipment operator. He returned home after a few weeks, explaining that he missed his wife and children, although his employers had been more than satisfied with his work and had made him an offer of a permanent job. Here is an instance of a young Inuit rejecting an opportunity for permanent employment in order to return to the land, and this in spite of the fact that he had several times told me he wished he could have a steady income so as to ensure that his family would not go hungry during lean times. His ties to the land were strong. Later that spring the three men from Aullativik who had worked at the mine the previous year were rehired, and one — Qamaniq — did accept training in the operation of heavy equipment. However, they all later returned to Aullativik.

Jimmy's refusal to continue with his job, despite its obvious economic advantages, is indicative of the behaviour of many Tununermiut males living in the camps in the early 1960s towards work "for the white man." Many, including some camp headmen, had worked in the past for Euro-Canadian agencies such as the RCMP and the HBC, in positions such as special constable and clerk. Almost all had returned to camp life and seemed to have rejected the outside world. These men had high status among the Tununermiut, both living in the settlement or in the camps. Their conscious choice of life on the land illustrates the tenacity of the contact-traditional life lived by the Tununermiut during that transitional and yet stable period.

THE COMING OF THE BUREAUCRATS

During the contact-traditional period, camp life for the Tununermiut continued in many respects as it had been for their ancestors, in spite of the many changes discussed in the previous chapter. In the early 1960s, although the settlement of Pond Inlet was the node of Tununermiut economic and religious activity and their link with the outside world, individual identity was rooted in camp residence. Inuit membership in a social unit was traditionally marked by a name — often a place-name — ending in the *-miut* suffix. The families who lived in camps in the Pond Inlet environs were known by their camp name, such as the Aullativikmiut of the camp in which I resided for most of my stay. Broader, more inclusive names were also employed, such as Tununermiut, which encompassed the people living in the settlement as well as all those in the outlying camps.

The Inuit name for Pond Inlet is Mittimatalik, and the few Inuit who lived there in the early 1960s were known as the Mittimatalikmiut. These were families who had one or more members in the employment of southern agencies, or had retired from such service and were unable to return to camp life because of poor health or age, as well as a few individuals who chose settlement life because of infirmities such as blindness or simply the proximity of close relatives who had regular employment with one of the agencies. In this chapter we shall examine the social and cultural patterns of the residents of Pond Inlet at the time of my first field trip to the area, and in the course of that examination will look at not only the Mittimatalikmiut but the Euro-Canadians and their agencies, as well as the interactions between the two. As we have seen, they were distinct and yet closely intertwined social groupings.

My initial insight into the social structure of the settlement was the realization that two social systems were present, the Mittimatalikmiut and the Euro-Canadian (and it was this that led me to move to a camp for my research). The Euro-Canadians formed a typical outpost of the type that anthropologists have met in colonial-like settings around the world. There were divisions within that community, and we shall examine them as well, but essentially they were a separate social unit from the settlement-dwelling Inuit. However, this segregation cannot be easily explained in terms of simplistic terms such as "racism," "prejudice," and so on. Discrimination did exist, and prejudicial attitudes toward Inuit were evident among some members of the Euro-Canadian community, but isolated instances are not an adequate explanation for the social separation between the two. Today, as will become apparent, Euro-Canadians are excluded from many Inuit activities in Pond Inlet, but neither can this pattern be tidily explained away by charges of racism against the Tununermiut. The situation was and is more complex than that, and we must look to historical factors if we are to understand it.

The Euro-Canadian Community and its Divisions

We have already dealt at some length with the histories of the three primary agencies in Pond Inlet; the police, missionaries, and traders. My own primary purpose in visiting the settlement was to study legal change, and so initially I concentrated on the police and the RCMP detachment as the expression of police activity. Nevertheless, circumstances made it both possible and desirable for me to interact with members of other agencies, in spite of my preference for avoiding excessive identification with Euro-Canadians in general. Whenever I visited the settlement with the Aullativikmiut I would stay overnight with the family of either the area administrator or the DNANR mechanic and would drop in at other Euro-Canadian homes. The hospitality I was always shown was gratefully accepted, for it gave me opportunities to gorge myself on "southern" foods, to have conversations in English, and to catch up on news of the outside world. At the homes where I stayed, I would first bathe in luxuriant warm water, trim my beard, and scrape from my teeth the black residue that was the result of continual tea drinking in the camp. Water was a scarce commodity in Inuit camps in winter, when the only source was chunks of ice melted over soapstone lamps.

When I left Aullativik in the following spring I lived for some time in the back room of an unoccupied student hostel, and in the summer rented a vacant teacherage. I felt that I was able to move comfortably between the different agencies in the settlement, although I had to be constantly on guard lest something I say be taken as supporting one side in a dispute between individuals or agencies. At times, even my silence was taken as tacit support for a position in an argument, and its proponent would later say that "the anthropologist agrees with me on this." Several of my Euro-Canadian friends must have thought that I had few opinions of my own.

To some extent I did become identified more than I cared for with the DNANR and its personnel, because of my overnight stays with them, but frequent dinner invitations to the home of the Anglican missionary, when his budget was so small that provision for a guest was almost a hardship, and the assistance the resident Catholic priest gave me in translating my questionnaire into Inuktitut, gave me some assurance that I was successful in crossing agency lines. I have already mentioned some of the ways in which the RCMP officer assisted me by helping me establish myself in a camp, and when in the settlement I shared many cups of coffee with the HBC manager in his home. I hope that they are all tolerant, should they read this, of my descriptions of the roles they performed in the day-to-day functioning of Pond Inlet as an outpost of southern life. And, I want to emphasize, the descriptions that follow will be of roles and the statuses to which they relate, not of personalities or individuals. Each incumbent of a position in the Euro-Canadian system of Pond Inlet in the 1960s had duties to perform that were unrelated to personal preferences and predilections. I made observations of role behaviour carried out by individuals, but I have tried to separate the role from the idiosyncracies of the individual. Occasional anecdotes will be used as illustrations, but they should not offend the persons who figure in them. The problems of such descriptions in settings where one individual is the incumbent of a specific status make for a serious ethical dilemma.

Although it has a different character today, Pond Inlet of the early 1960s was essentially a service centre ministering to the real and manufactured needs of the Tununermiut. Increasingly, it has become a centre programmed to service the Euro-Canadians who live there as well, but that is a later story. Put in broad terms, the services that Euro-Canadian agencies sought to provide were of a material, spiritual, and intellectual nature. Not all of them were interested in making profound changes in traditional Inuit society and culture, but rather in making modifications when relevant to their own mandates. We discussed this earlier in terms of the police, traders, and missionaries: the needs that they saw themselves as satisfying were often spurious or manufactured. The Inuit had, for example, developed through contact with whalers and traders, needs for ammunition, traps, cloth, and foodstuffs, and the HBC provided for those needs. On an ideological level, however, the representatives of the Euro-Canadian agencies saw themselves as provisioners of a new and, from their perspective, superior way of life. This was the overt rationale for their presence in the Canadian Arctic. From the vantage point of revisionist history it is easy to criticize the contact agents of the 1960s. They were indeed exploitative in many respects, and had hidden motives. No matter how much the HBC may claim that it operated in the Arctic for benevolent reasons, and that in later years it did so at a cost to itself, the fact remains that it established posts in order to obtain furs and skins to meet southern and European market demands. The police were there to enforce Canadian law, and thus to reinforce Canadian sovereignty in its Arctic lands, and the missionaries offered a new religion and sought to stamp out shamanism. Nevertheless, I am personally convinced that the agents in the field generally believed they were offering assistance of one type or another to the Inuit. Their personal motivations were decent.

There were five Euro-Canadian agencies located in Pond Inlet in the 1960s: Anglican and Roman Catholic missions, an RCMP detachment, an HBC store, and a recently established DNANR contingent. The first four had been there for decades, and had limited goals for social and cultural change. The upstart DNANR had more grandiose purposes in mind, and became a major catalyst of change. After its inception, this agency of the federal government was to wield what were potentially dictatorial powers in the Northwest Territories, and its personnel were responsible for overseeing and in many instances directing everything from the development of mineral resources to the day-to-day lives of the Inuit under its jurisdiction. The goal they established for themselves, with the blessing of the government of the time, was nothing less than the complete integration of the Canadian Inuit population into the fabric of Canadian society, and policies and programs were aimed at this goal. The basic policy was concisely stated two years after the creation of the department by Jean Lesage (1955), then minister of northern affairs and national resources:

> The objective of Government policy is relatively easy to define. It is to give the Eskimo the same rights, privileges, opportunities and responsibilities of all other Canadians: in short, to enable them to share fully in the national life of Canada. It is pointless to consider whether the Eskimo was happier before the white man came, for the white man has come and time

cannot be reversed. The only realistic approach is to accept the fact that the Eskimo will be brought evermore under the influences of civilization to the south. The task, then, is to help him adjust his life and his thoughts to all that the encroachment of this new life must mean.

As one senior member of the Department is reputed to have stated, the Inuit were to be brought from the Stone Age to the atomic age in one generation. The axe had fallen, and the contact-traditional period faced a major threat to its existence. The Inuit were to be "modernized," for better or worse. As the first step in the implementation of this policy a Northern Service Officer (NSO) was stationed in Pond Inlet, to be followed by teachers, mechanics, and, in time, nurses.

In 1963 there were four full-time Euro-Canadian personnel attached to the DNANR contingent in Pond Inlet (three with families) and several Inuit who were employed on a part- or full-time basis. The original NSO had been replaced that year by an area administrator, whose position had a higher civil service ranking. A single teacher had come and gone, to be replaced by a married man and a single woman. The fourth member was the equipment mechanic, whose responsibilities included maintenance of the powerhouse, supervision of Inuit workers, and other assorted tasks.

At the time, area administrators in northern communities were often uncertain of the precise nature of their mandate and duties. For example, the resident administrator told me that "most of my work isn't laid down in black and white ... my actual duties are pretty vague." He and others like him had been given crash courses in the south before taking up their positions, but the training received was inadequate. Some education in Inuktitut received at the "northern college," as the preparatory training program was called, was an asset but not extensive enough for work among monolingual Inuktitut speakers, which most Inuit of that period were. Vallee (1962) had identified the lack of precision in role definition for NSOs in Baker Lake some years earlier:

> The position of the community with the least clearly defined function is that of the NSO. He is told that he is the senior government representative in the community, but what this implies in specific terms is not clear.

Vallee had juxtaposed the role of NSO/area administrator with those of other government personnel in a settlement, such as police had to be respected and maintained, while at the same time the senior civil servant had been instructed to do whatever possible to produce the "modernization" sought by his[1] own department. The lack of precise directives could be a major asset for imaginative and innovative administrators, as evidenced by James Houston's development of the embryonic Inuit art industry in Cape Dorset in the 1950s. Houston presumably regarded his mandate as being to develop a new settlement-based economy, and he was given relatively free rein to use his own experiences as an artist to create a cadre of local artists. The rest, of course, is Arctic history.

The resident NSO or administrator, then, was expected to produce results with little specific direction, and to create visible evidence of them in the form of innovative programs, and hardware such as buildings and technological expansion, and yet was monitored by higher-ranking officials and committees to the south. Failure to produce such proof could lead to criticism and possibly loss of the position. On the other hand, the NSO or administrator could do virtually nothing without administrative approval from, for example, Frobisher Bay (now Iqaluit), the administrative centre for DNANR in the eastern Arctic, and this in turn had to be ratified by more senior officials in Ottawa. The difficulty was compounded by diversification and autonomy of department branches, which often had conflicting policies. Acceptance of a new program by one would often be countered by rejection by another. In addition, in the early 1960s communication between isolated settlements and administrative centres such as Frobisher Bay was poor. If an administrator did not want to entrust a message to radio, which could be monitored by anyone with a receiving set, he was forced to rely on the mail, and mail service into settlements such as Pond Inlet was infrequent and dependent on the whims of individual pilots. Often there would be no flights in for as much as three months at a time, and even then, if a craft had a heavy load, it might not take the mail, despite the fact that a pilot who left the mail behind was in no way certain of a bed for the night or even a cup of coffee in the settlement. Hence, most pilots tried to bring along a bottle of whisky for their hosts as well as the mail.

An example might illustrate the problems of an administrator wishing to make visible progress in fulfilling his mandate while also being at a loss how best to do so. As the only facilities for bathing in the settlement were in the homes of the Euro-Canadians, who had bathtubs and large holding tanks for melting ice, shortly after his arrival the administrator decided that a community sauna bath was needed. (The Inuit living in the settlement had government provided housing, but although most had small bathrooms they had no plumbing. The bathrooms were often used to store meat.) The administrator was aware that saunas had a long history of use among the Sammi of northern Scandinavia, and thought that they might be culturally acceptable to the Inuit. Scrap lumber was used in the construction of the sauna, which had an attached room equipped with a washing machine for the women of the community to use. (Each Euro-Canadian home had equipment for washing clothes.) The men of the settlement were sent out to search along the shoreline for rocks of the proper consistency and with the appropriate heating qualities. Finally the sauna was completed, and the administrator invited several Mittimatalikmiut men to join him in testing it. I happened to be visiting the settlement on the inaugural day, and was invited to take part. There was no thermometer attached to the wall, as one usually finds in more conventional saunas and Turkish baths in the south, and none of us participating were aware of how hot the room had become. No one was surprised, though, when one of the men suddenly bolted from the sauna and made for the nearest snowbank, followed by several others. Although the Pond Inlet sauna was a noble effort and was in future used by a few men, although at less extreme temperatures, it never received full community support. It was gone when I returned a decade later.

The problems faced by administrators, such as an inadequate job description and the complexities that the DNANR bureaucracy presented, were essentially problems for the individual incumbent (but did affect the rate and patterns of change within the settlement and its environs). Despite these problems, however, there were certain well-defined attributes attached to the position of administrator. The administrator was, as mentioned before, the senior civil servant and government representative in his settlement, and as such "directed" the DNANR operations. Although he was an employee of the federal government, he also represented the Government of the Northwest Territories, and occasionally the two positions would conflict. Most of his day-to-day activities were related to his Territorial position. For example, in what was intended to improve the local economies and provide a better quality of life, the Territorial government sold boats and rented houses to the Inuit, and the administrator was agent for such transactions. In his position as representative of the Territorial government he was also responsible for bulk sales of fuel oil, the enforcement of dog ordinances in the settlement, and the management of fur exports. At times, the exercise of these responsibilities conflicted with activities traditionally carried out by police, such as the enforcement of dog ordinances. It was required that dogs in the settlement be continually chained, but camp people visiting Pond Inlet often neglected to chain their animals, allowing them to run free. The resident administrator had to handle the potential conflict over jurisdiction with tact if he did not want to create tensions between himself and the RCMP officer.

Another area of conflict was the provision of social assistance. As Canadian citizens, the Tununermiut were eligible to receive family allowance and Old Age Security payments. Historically these payments were handled by the RCMP, but by the early 1960s they had in most settlements been taken over by administrators or NSOs, as were relief and welfare payments and special forms of social assistance such as pensions to the blind. Occasionally indigent, disabled, or elderly persons were provided with heavily subsidized housing, and decisions about eligibility were made by administrators. These had all formerly been handled by the RCMP, and the inevitable inter-agency conflict was created when they were taken over by DNANR personnel. The traditional base of the RCMP in the area was obviously threatened by the usurping of their responsibilities.

Although not explicitly directed to do so, NSOs and administrators were encouraged to develop local consumer co-operatives and community councils. Neither existed in Pond Inlet in 1963, but the resident administrator worked towards the development of both. He had previous experience with the very successful co-operative venture at Cape Dorset, where he had been an NSO before being promoted and stationed at Pond Inlet. Administrators like him were also encouraged to improve Inuit housing, in both settlements and camps. A program to provide government-subsidized housing had been initiated in Pond Inlet by his predecessor, and he expanded on it. He would investigate potential recipients and work out financial arrangements with those considered worthy. (I was never certain how these decisions were made, and it is interesting to speculate on whether the concept of worthiness held by the administrator coincided with that subscribed to by the Inuit themselves.) Under the housing program, a few dwellings were constructed in camps, but most were built in the settlement itself — one of the first steps towards what I term "centralization."

The administrator also attempted to encourage group purchases of large Peterhead boats, which, it was assumed, would improve the local economy by expanding summer hunting territories and creating more efficient hunting crews. The assumption was based on experiences in other settlements. However, in Pond Inlet only one sale was made, and it was made to an individual. Kayak, who had worked for the RCMP for several years as a special constable (in fact, he received the Order of Canada for his services to the RCMP), had put away enough savings to make a substantial down payment. He was to later use the boat as a charter craft for scientific teams and hunting parties from the south.

The duties and responsibilities of the administrator were, then, primarily of an economic nature. New housing and employment opportunities in the settlement were over time to attract camp people to it as a place of residence. But if the Inuit were to be thrust into the atomic age in one generation, education would have to be the prime mechanism. The two enthusiastic teachers who arrived in Pond Inlet in the summer of 1963 to manage the operations of the federal day school were quick to take up the challenge. The woman taught the first grade in the central room of one of the newly constructed student hostels, and her male colleague taught the higher elementary grades in the one-room schoolhouse. There was an expectable clustering of pupils in the lower grades. The main classroom activity for both teachers was the development of English-language skills. In fact, many parents allowed their children to attend school mainly because they felt the youngsters needed to acquire such skills. (They were also motivated by the impression that if they withheld their offspring from school their family allowance cheques, an important stable source of income, would be discontinued.) The effectiveness of instruction was hindered by the inability of either teacher to speak Inuktitut. Teacher turnover was rapid: with some notable exceptions, few teachers during the first decade of DNANR-sponsored education in the Canadian Arctic spent enough time in the field to acquire more than the most rudimentary command of Inuktitut. Some teachers in later years did benefit by participating in a summer language course held yearly in Rankin Inlet and sponsored by the University of Saskatchewan, but these were a small number of committed individuals who had opted for prolonged Arctic residence.

The two teachers in Pond Inlet in 1963 carried out several community activities above and beyond their basic nine-to-four duties. The woman taught evening classes in English for adults, and the man organized a Boy Scout troop. Both also attempted, at least initially, to encourage Inuit children and adults to visit their homes in the evenings and on weekends. This was to produce difficulties for the woman when Inuit men misinterpreted her hospitality, but the misunderstanding was overcome by tactful explanations on both sides. There had been a long history of sexual alliances between Inuit women and Euro-Canadian men going back to the whaling period, and perhaps Inuit males had interpreted the friendly overtures of Euro-Canadian females in terms of that history. Also, it was perhaps a simple matter for Inuit males to interpret friendliness on the part of Euro-Canadian women as having sexual connotations, given the degree of sexual freedom in traditional Inuit society. (I intentionally use the term "freedom" rather than "promiscuity," for this freedom existed within well-defined cultural parameters.) In the 1990s the educational picture has changed dramatically in Pond Inlet, as a generation of youth who progressed through high school have re-entered the community structure.

The resident equipment mechanic was the fourth member of the DNANR contingent, and in some ways he had the most power of any of them, although in the civil service hierarchy he had the lowest status. It has often been said in a not completely joking way that mechanics "run" northern settlements, and the statement was true in the 1960s in a more than strictly mechanical sense. The duties related to the position were several and diverse. For example, the mechanic was responsible for the maintenance of the powerhouse and the generator housed within it, which was the community's source of electricity. He kept the heating systems of the DNANR buildings in good operation; supervised the retrieval of ice from offshore icebergs during winter months, when these provided the only source of fresh water; and maintained DNANR heavy equipment and vehicles such as tractors and bombardiers.

The mechanic also had extensive day-to-day contact with several Inuit who worked under his supervision. These were men who performed the tasks of ice retrieval, collection of garbage and toilet bags, road maintenance, house construction, and so on. The Inuit were not accustomed to office work, and the mechanic was the only Euro-Canadian who did much of his own work out of doors. His practical skills were ones that Inuit males envied, and that they could observe him using. The administrator had more authority than the mechanic, but the Tununermiut of the time had little understanding of the bureaucracy that legitimized and supported it. The former was seen as a "paper shuffler," while the mechanic's activities were perceived as "authentic." In essence, the mechanic was the main role model for Tununermiut males who aspired to positions in the Euro-Canadian structure. I am convinced that he was the major agent of acculturation, despite the paradoxical fact that he was the Euro-Canadian least recognized as an acculturating influence. Many of the men who worked for him did acquire skills that would stand them in good stead at a later time, but they also perhaps developed particular attitudes towards the values of the larger society of which they were not a part, because of interaction with a particular resident mechanic.

The administrator, the male teacher, and the mechanic were all married with young children and tended to form a social cluster of their own to which the female teacher was only peripherally connected. Being single, she did not share the domestic role of her colleagues and acted in many respects as a liaison between the DNANR and members of other Euro-Canadian agencies. Occasional parties, such as New Year's Eve gatherings, brought together all Euro-Canadians, and work-related activities brought individuals into contact with one another, but basically the DNANR employees formed a group of their own. This may in part have been a defensive response to covert hostility expressed towards them by other Euro-Canadians who resented their presence, although perhaps not on a personal level, and what they perceived as imperialistic objectives and behaviour. DNANR encroachment on the jurisdictions of others was certainly resented, and this resentment was recognized by DNANR personnel. Other Euro-Canadians, such as the trader and missionaries, were also deeply disturbed by the openly change-oriented objectives of the DNANR.

The missionaries represented a second Euro-Canadian tentacle into the lives of the Tununermiut from the large social organism to the south. In many respects, the missions in Pond Inlet were similar to proselytizing missions around the world. Both the Roman Catholic and Anglican missionaries saw their role as being to minister to the spiritual condition of the Tununermiut. Here I will depart from my attempt to preserve anonymity by mentioning that the resident Catholic priest of long standing was the well-known and highly respected archaeologist Father Guy-Marie Rousseliere. Father Rousseliere left the settlement shortly after my arrival to act as technical consultant to the crew filming the critically acclaimed series on the Netsilik Inuit at Pelly Bay. While at Pelly Bay he was involved in a serious accident, and as a consequence was hospitalized in the south for most of the following year. An itinerant priest was sent to Pond Inlet to minister to his single-family parish. (Although the Catholic church had been established in the settlement decades before, a few years earlier all converts had moved to Igloolik, leaving one family behind.)

In spite of their small parish, Father Rousseliere and his replacement were extremely influential among the Tununermiut, both Catholic and Protestant. Each man had years of Arctic experience behind him — Father Rousseliere had spent a considerable amount of time living in camps, as both priest and archaeologist — and each was fluent in Inuktitut. This extensive experience was the basis of the high degree of respect the two also received from their fellow Euro-Canadians.

In short, the two priests had one of the main factors in northern prestige-acquisition: lengthy residence. In the early 1960s, at least, recent arrivals had to work hard to earn respect from Euro-Canadians as well as the Inuit. This was one of the problems that DNANR personnel faced in carving out a niche for themselves in settlement power structures.

The priests I met in Pond Inlet had such experience, or credentials. Anglican Inuit from the camps rarely visited the settlement without making a social call at the Catholic mission, in spite of admonitions from earlier Anglican missionaries that the tall statue of Jesus on the cross standing on the hill above the Catholic mission was a symbol of the devil. (I was told of this by several of my Inuit informants.) The Tununermiut regarded the priests as friends who understood and respected their traditional culture, but personal accounts written by the first missionaries in the area reveal in often florid prose the bitter struggles between the two missions for the souls of the Tununermiut, and these must have been confusing and more to the Inuit themselves. Much of the antagonism between the two had disappeared by the 1960s, but I often wondered how the Inuit had handled the conceptual problems of being presented with two apparently opposed images of the same faith.

The incumbent Anglican missionary was at a disadvantage the year that I arrived, even with his large congregation, for it was the first year of his tour of duty in the Arctic. Recently arrived from England with his wife and infant daughter, he was unable to speak Inuktitut and yet was expected to carry on an active weekly program of services, meetings, and family visits. Nevertheless, by assuming the mantle of the Anglican missionary in the area, he soon became possibly the pivotal person in the Euro-Canadian community, at least in the view of most Tununermiut. As I have mentioned, shamanism was still alive among them, and the last remaining shaman, at least to the best of my knowledge, was also a practising and devout Anglican. The missionary once proudly showed me an inlaid seal-skin rug that had been donated to him for use in the new chapel he planned to build — donated by the shaman. On another occasion, I recall Kadloo, one of the Aullativikmiut, telling me that his brother in Pond Inlet was very ill and that he thought the shaman had placed a spell on him. Kadloo planned to travel to the settlement to ask the missionary to invoke the spirit of Jesus Christ to counteract the power of the shaman. It seemed to me that Tununermiut like Kadloo regarded the missionary as a particularly powerful shaman who had, in Jesus, a spirit helper superior to those of other shamans. Certainly shamanism had been a central structure underlying traditional Inuit culture, and so the influence of the missionary seen as shaman is not difficult to comprehend.

A third Euro-Canadian agency in the settlement was the Hudson's Bay Company trading post, which at the time was staffed by a trader from Scotland who had a decade or so of Arctic experience. The HBC store had, until the arrival of DNANR, been the centre for Tununermiut economic involvement with the outside world. The physical complex consisted of the store, which was a fairly large single room with a small office and storage space attached at the rear, several warehouses, and the manager's residence. Like many HBC managers, the resident trader spoke Inuktitut fluently. Most day-to-day purchases in the store were handled by the Inuit clerk, but the manager could usually be found there as well, bartering over fur prices, greeting visitors from the camps, or working on the accounts. It was he who told Inuit men the value of their furs and skins and what goods could be purchased with them, and many of their informants told me that they believed he was the one who set prices. They had little awareness in the 1960s of fluctuating southern markets, and so regarded the trader as a person of considerable influence over their lives and economic well-being. Because of his fluency in their language, he was in close touch with camp activities and gossip. He was also the local justice of the peace but had few opportunities to appear in that role.

As was common in virtually all communities in the Canadian Arctic, the HBC store in Pond Inlet served as both a social and an economic centre. Almost every woman in the settlement — Inuit or Euro-Canadian — made at least one visit to it every day, often regardless of whether she had any specific purchases in mind. At any time of day, if it was open, clusters of people could be found standing about talking in the store or on the front steps. Camp people would usually drive their dogs up onto the ice in front of the store and go in for a visit (and to warm themselves) before they had even unpacked their gear boxes. (Gear boxes were discarded produce containers that would be tied onto the rear of a sled and used to carry the tea kettle, the primus stove, often a hunk of bannock, and any other items the traveller wanted easily accessible.) Because the manager was usually in the store, and so physically present even if largely socially invisible at such times, he was often the first Euro-Canadian to pick up news from the camps.

I will discuss the RCMP detachment at somewhat greater length than the others because it was the agency that concerned me most that year. Another reason for giving it special attention, however, is that the police had more of an acculturative influence on camp life of the time than did other Euro-Canadians, and this influence extended beyond the strictly legal. The Pond Inlet detachment had originally been a centre for police activity in the entire region of the high northeastern Arctic, after its establishment following the Janes case. It had been staffed with several constables and officers, but in 1963 there was only the one officer in residence for most of the year, even though it was still the administrative centre for northern Baffin Island, with jurisdiction over Clyde River to the east and Arctic Bay to the west.

As suggested earlier, the responsibilities of RCMP personnel in the Arctic, at least before the development of the DNANR, were varied and extended far beyond the limited role of peace officer. They were succinctly put by Van Norman (1951: 111), a former officer who served a term in Pond Inlet in the early 1950s:

> At this post the RCMP is the only Government department stationed, and consequently upon its personnel fall the duties which other Government departments require performed. Family allowance and old age pension administration, reporting on game conditions, registration of births, deaths and marriages, post office, issuing coal mining permits, collecting royalties on exporting furs, issuing general hunting licenses, recording weather, plus the normal duties involving enforcement of the Northwest Territories Ordinances and Criminal Code, patrolling by dog teams to various Eskimo camps to determine native living conditions, and such remaining duties which the Government deems advisable to enforce.

Van Norman went on to say that his own duties as a law enforcement officer were limited because the local Inuit were, in his words, "fairly self reliant, law abiding people". A similar sentiment was expressed by one of his predecessors, who stated in 1931 that "the Eskimos are a kindly people and perfectly all right if you treat them decently" (Robertson, 1934: 186). These are quite different views from that expressed by the individual who had urged missionization of the Inuit to make them into honest traders.

The normal activities and duties of resident police in Pond Inlet changed very little between the time of Van Norman's writing and the advent of the DNANR. The NSO who established the Pond Inlet DNANR operation had apparently been hesitant to appropriate the many non-police duties of the RCMP in the settlement, but his successor was convinced that they were part of his mandate, and so he assumed responsibility for such matters as the administration of welfare payments and the issuing of coal licences shortly after his arrival. (The Tununermiut had for several decades mined a small deposit of soft coal located on the Salmon River, five or so miles from the settlement, and sold it to the HBC and the RCMP. This was terminated in 1965 because of the ready availability of other forms of fuel.) The police's resentment of these actions has already been mentioned.

The registration of what anthropologists term "life crises," such as births, deaths, and marriages, continued to be the responsibility of the police, and when a missionary was not in residence they might actually perform a marriage ceremony. They also kept current the "disc list" for the area, a yearly listing of all Inuit families and individuals in the district along with the number assigned to each one as an identifying marker for bureaucratic purposes. The Inuit traditionally had several personal names, some of which were secret, but did not use family or surnames. The list, which many Euro-Canadian observers considered de-humanizing in its impersonality, allowed police and others to keep track of individuals.

The RCMP were servants of the federal government, although they were expected to also enforce ordinances of the Government of the Northwest Territories. In 1963, however, a new ordinance authorized the commissioner of the NWT to actually contract for the services of the RCMP. Formally titled the Royal Canadian Mounted Police Agreement Ordinance, it stated that

> the commissioner may, on behalf of the Government of the Northwest Territories, enter into an agreement with the Government of Canada, under and for the purposes of the Royal Canadian Mounted Police Act, to provide for the use of or employment of the Royal Canadian Mounted Police, or a portion thereof, in aiding the administration of justice in the Territories, and in carrying into effect the laws in force therein upon such terms and conditions as may be contained in the agreement. (Ordinances of the Northwest Territories, 1963: 82)

In practice, aside from extremely infrequent serious crimes such as murder, most laws enforced by the RCMP in the eastern Arctic were Territorial ordinances such as the game laws and public health ordinances, and with most of the Tununermiut still living in camps little energy was expended in enforcing even these. (Game and public health ordinances when violated, were violated in a camp area, far removed from the eyes of the police.) One of the resident RCMP officers in 1963 gave the following response when I asked him about criminal problems among the Tununermiut:

> There is no crime here at all. Of course, there are some laws which the Eskimos have difficulty in understanding, and so break. For example, they aren't too good about tying up their dogs when they're in the settlement. You've seen dogs running around loose. The same is true of some of the game laws. They had trouble understanding them, but now they know and observe them. They are very trustworthy. For example, I like to keep a record of how many caribou there are in any given area. I want to know how many hunters have hunted any one herd, so I've asked the men to tell me when they hunt caribou and tell me where they're going. Then, when someone comes in and tells me that he is going hunting, I can suggest that he not hunt in a certain place because it has been over-hunted. Now, the people keep record on their own. They are quick to understand the idea of conservation. The best I have ever heard of. (Personal communication)

This particular officer, who had been stationed in Pond Inlet for several years, had what might be termed a liberal attitude towards law enforcement. He recognized the importance of what anthropologists have called customary law, and made use of it when imposing sanctions on violators of not-too-serious ordinances. For example, he tried to take into account the circumstances under which a violation occurred, and whether it seemed to be reasonable behaviour in traditional Inuit terms. Also, he often employed traditional sanctions rather than formally charging an individual. Shaming was a traditional form of sanction, and he might approach a man in a camp who was known to have violated some ordinances and "call him down" in front of his peers.

This pattern of interpreting Canadian laws in terms of traditional practices had been established by precedent through the court decisions of Justice Jack Sissons, the first justice of the Territorial Court of the Northwest Territories, and continued in the late 1960s through the tenure of his successor, Justice William Morrow. Justice Morrow once told me that he tried to avoid sending an Inuk to a southern prison, because in his opinion there were no hardened Inuit criminals and he did not want to "produce the first one." (personal communication).

The resident officer in Pond Inlet went on leave for an extended period of time in 1964, and his temporary replacement took a far more formal and orthodox approach to law enforcement. This, I believe, exemplifies the problems of having one individual fill a specific position, such as that of police officer. Changing role behaviour in specific positions must have been confusing for the Inuit in their attempts to understand Canadian institutions.

However, criminal activities as defined by Canadian law were indeed infrequent among the Tununermiut in the early 1960s, and the police officers' time was taken up with other duties not usually thought of as central to the police role. Perhaps the most important of these was in the medical realm. There was a small nursing station in Pond Inlet but no resident nurse, and the nearest hospital was in Frobisher Bay, far to the south. The police had offered lay medical service to Inuit in both camps and the settlement for decades, and occasionally even acted as midwives in cases of difficult births. They had been instructed in basic medical skills during their RCMP training, and built on that through practical experience in the field. The officer in Pond Inlet would deliver medical kits consisting of bandages, ointments, and so on to all camps on his periodic tours of them, and explain to the headmen how the contents were to be used. (This was not always a successful exercise. Accidents were common in Inuit camps, as they are in any setting where small children are found. I recall watching the contents of one such kit, which had been delivered to Aullativik, used up within two weeks. Every bloody nose or scratched knee received prompt and thorough attention during that brief period, but thereafter such minor emergencies were left to the healing powers of nature until a new kit was delivered.) When anyone in a camp or the settlement was involved in an accident, was seriously ill, or had trouble with pregnancy or an impending birth, friends or relatives would make every effort possible to bring them to the police detachment for assistance, or would send a message to the police, confident that if weather conditions permitted, a house call would be made. If the matter was extremely serious, the police would attempt to have an aircraft sent in from Frobisher Bay to evacuate the individual. Weather conditions often made this impossible, however, and in those instances the police acted as lay medical practitioners.

The activities of the police in Pond Inlet before the arrival of the DNANR were obviously diverse, then, with actual law enforcement being only a small part. With the DNANR legally usurping many of their responsibilities in the early 1960s, it is under-standable that the RCMP came to be known, and indeed to consider themselves, as "the forgotten men of the Arctic." I heard police officers use the expression in wry if not bitter tones on more than one occasion. Increasingly their role was to become primarily that of a symbol of Canadian sovereignty in its Arctic regions. At the same time, with centralization and rapid change, their function as police would also increasingly be called into play.

The Mittimatalikmiut

Ostensibly, the Euro-Canadian agencies in Pond Inlet were there to provide services for the Inuit, even though the Inuit had survived for a millenium or so without those services. But the Euro-Canadians were in what was for them an alien environment, and so they in turn required the services of Inuit workers to maintain their operations. A few Tununermiut lived in the settlement be-cause of infirmities or advanced age, but most of the Mittimatalik-miut worked for Euro-Canadians. The only agency that did not have at least one paid Inuit employee was the Roman Catholic mission, but every Inuit in the area was ready to offer assistance to the Catholic missionary if it was needed.

The Anglican mission had an Inuk serving as catechist. He sup-ported himself and his family primarily through hunting, but also worked part-time for the missionary. His duties, beyond assisting in services, were to provide food (obtained through hunting) for the mission dogteam; act as a guide for the missionary when he visited camps or Arctic Bay, which was also an Anglican settlement but did not have a resident minister; and to carry out menial tasks such as disposing of the mission garbage and toilet bags and keep-ing the coal bin filled. Jimmy Muckpah became the catechist shortly after I left Pond Inlet in the summer of 1964, and so began what was to be a rapid process culminating in his ordination three years later as an Anglican priest. He received his theological training in Pangnirtung.

Two Inuit men worked for the RCMP as special constables. Their functions were basically to act as guides and orderlies for the Euro-Canadian constables. They were issued modified versions of the RCMP uniform (or, at least, the materials, which would be made into garments by their wives) and were provided with private houses. The latter were located adjacent to the detachment, which housed the Euro-Canadian police. One of the special constables, the well-known Kayak, was a Tununermiut who had worked with the force for almost twenty years. Kayak was attached to several different detachments during his time with the RCMP before he returned to his own people. His fellow special constable was an individual from Port Harrison who had been stationed at Grise Fiord before being transferred to Pond Inlet. (Grise Fiord is a settlement on Ellesmere Island that comprises Inuit from Pond Inlet and Port Harrison. The Port Harrison people were relocated there ostensibly because of game shortages in their indigenous area, with those from Pond Inlet being brought in to teach them to hunt in the high Arctic terrain. The Port Harrison people have charged that more political motives were behind the federal government's decision to use them as the basis for a high Arctic settlement at a time when Canadian sovereignty in the northern regions was being challenged.)

The special constable from Port Harrison found himself and his family to be rather socially isolated from the Tununermiut, although they did form alliances with some of the latter. This, I believe, was an expression of traditional Inuit ethnicity. It was difficult for individuals from one of the more embrasive *miut* groups to accept people whose identity was with an external *miut* group. Several years later I observed this same manifestation of what the sociologists term "boundary maintenance" in Rankin Inlet, which had been settled by families brought in from a number of different settlement areas. They tended to maintain their social distance from one another. Kayak's home, in contrast to that of his co-worker, was almost always filled with visitors from camps who were in the settlement to trade or for other reasons, and with Mittimatalikmiut.

A retired special constable, Joe Panikpakutsuk, also lived in the settlement with his family. Because of a frozen lung suffered while still with the RCMP he was unable to endure the rigours of camp life. Joe's daughter was a local celebrity at the time, for she was the announcer for a CBC Inuktitut radio program, which was received every Wednesday evening and brought all other activities to a standstill as people congregated about radios to listen attentively. I felt that Joe walked a figurative tightrope, in that he seemed to want to express his Inuit male identity while at the same time, given that he was a settlement dweller without formal employment, that status was in some respects questionable. There were several other former special constables in the area, but they all lived in the camps; I believe that it was important for them to re-establish their Inuit identities after long periods of identification with a Euro-Canadian agency.

The Bay's full-time Inuit clerk, Mercosak, had worked for the company for several years and was still with it when I returned ten years later. His home was on the edge of the settlement, and like Kayak's was almost always filled with visitors. He and his wife were genial hosts. The resident manager was unmarried, and an Inuit woman worked as housekeeper in his residence while her husband had casual employment doing jobs about the HBC complex. Along with these employees, usually two or more men would be found making repairs to buildings, transporting goods from one of the warehouses to the store, and doing other work on a part-time basis. These casual labourers were usually camp men who would return to their camps when their employment terminated. Each year before sealift several women would be hired to pack seal skins for transportation to the south on the supply ship.

These positions were semi-traditional ones; they had existed for several decades. The Bay, the RCMP, and the missionaries had always needed Inuit to assist them in their activities. This employment picture was to change dramatically with the arrival of the DNANR, however, although in 1963 there was only one full-time employee of the agency whose long-term job security seemed viable. This was Danielee, a twenty-four-year-old man who had been sent "out," to use the Arctic expression, to receive training in the south as a heavy equipment operator. He had been hired by the first NSO to be stationed in Pond Inlet, and when he was hired it was anticipated that in time he would be promoted to assistant NSO. As such he would work closely with either an NSO or an area administrator. He was originally, then, destined to become a bureaucrat, but this was not to transpire. The administrator who replaced the NSO decided that Danielee was too young for the position and was too lacking in political influence. The promotion did not happen, and the same administrator described Danielee's position as being that of "simply a tractor driver and maintenance man." He worked under the direct supervision of the Euro-Canadian mechanic, and if he did not have prestige beforehand, he surely acquired it from his work with heavy equipment and his association with the individual whose skills were so admired by other Tununermiut.

In spite of his missed promotion, Danielee was the highest-paid Inuit in the settlement. He and his young family lived in a relatively spacious DNANR house that was the equal, in terms of floor space and furnishings, of several of those inhabited by Euro-Canadians. As a full-time employee of DNANR, he received, along with his salary, the same size of yearly food ration as Euro-Canadian employees, although its composition reflected somewhat different food preferences. Danielee supplemented the ration with large food purchases from Frobisher Bay and Montreal, sent in by aircraft. Danielee truly walked a thin line, for he was employed by, and so identified with, the upstart DNANR, and yet he and his wife were rarely invited to attend the larger social functions held at the homes of his Euro-Canadian co-workers. Even when such invitations were extended, they were rarely accepted — he or his wife would find a convenient excuse for not attending. (They were privately invited to the home of the administrator frequently, but that was different from attending, or being invited to attend, the larger gatherings.) Danielee may not have had much political influence, but it was very important to him that his social position within the Tununermiut society be retained. A major reason for the large expenditures on food was to enable him and his wife to lavishly entertain camp people visiting the settlement. He often found himself in difficulty with both the mechanic and the administrator for sleeping late after all-night gatherings at his home of land people who were not bound by Euro-Canadian work routines. In summer in particular, as the midnight sun circled the sky, Tununermiut would ignore the diurnal cycle, and Danielee was often caught between two worlds in his attempt to stand with a foot in both.

At the same time two other men were working on a full-time but nevertheless temporary basis for DNANR, and it had been anticipated that eventually both would be given permanent employment. One, who was the son of a camp headman who had worked for the RCMP as a special constable twenty or so years earlier, was being trained to take on the position of assistant to the administrator that had been denied Danielee. In the meantime, his actual duties were largely menial, consisting of disposing of toilet and garbage bags from homes and offices and picking up after the mechanic and Danielee. The administrator described his diverse tasks in the following way:

> His job is to take care of the garbage, sewage and do carpentry and other jobs. He's also the school janitor. He writes letters for me in Eskimo, distributes family allowance cheques to the settlement people, fetches people for me when I want them, and acts as a spy for me. You know, he tells me where people are, what they are doing, and so on. (Personal communication)

Tragically, before Kaunak had completed his first year of employment, and before he could take on the promotion, he died at the age of thirty of a heart disorder. He was replaced by one of the most politically powerful men among the Tununermiut. Maktar was the male head of the only Roman Catholic family in the area, and had in the past been a highly respected camp headman. His appointment was to have major consequences for later political developments in the settlement.

The other full-time DNANR employee had originally been hired as the school janitor, but official confirmation of this had not been received from the regional headquarters in Frobisher Bay by the time I left the field. He did some janitorial work and also assisted on a crew involved in constructing a power line through the settlement. Other individuals were hired sporadically to work on construction crews and at other activities. All three full-time Inuit employees were provided with DNANR housing, for which they paid relatively low rents. Danielee had ordered a large three-bedroom house for himself, however, which was expected to arrive on the 1964 sealift.

The DNANR was involved that year in rapid expansion of their facilities, and for most of the fall and winter a crew of four Euro-Canadian tradesmen and their foreman lived in the settlement while working on the construction of a school, two student hostels, and a new house for the equipment mechanic. For two months a crew of three men joined the group while building the first road through the settlement. The foreman of the first crew arrived several weeks before his men, and during that time used Inuit workers. A sensitive individual who was committed to northern living, he worked hard to train the Inuit, in the short time available, in carpentry and other skills. They were mainly camp people, and returned to the land as soon as the regular crew arrived.

Camp children who attended the federal day school in Pond Inlet required accommodation during the school year; to meet this need the DNANR provided the two hostels mentioned earlier, although only one of them was used that year. An Inuit couple had been hired to act as hostel parents; the wife prepared meals and her husband worked as caretaker.

Finally, young girls living in the settlement often worked as babysitters for Euro-Canadian families, and a few older women found part-time employment as domestics in Euro-Canadian homes.

Relations Between Tununermiut and Euro-Canadians

I have already identified some of the contexts in which social interaction between camp people, Mittimatalikmiut, and Euro-Canadians occurred. These were limited, and to a considerable extent institutionalized or at least formalized, possibly to the comfort of both Inuit and Euro-Canadians. More informal relationships also took place, of course. Sexual liaisons between Inuit women and Euro-Canadian men had long been common, and the pattern continued, although perhaps more discreetly. For example, there were occasions when Euro-Canadians working on construction crews were summarily "sent south" by the RCMP or their employers because of alleged sexual involvements with under-aged Inuit women.

For a settlement such as Pond Inlet to function, information had to flow back and forth between the Inuit and Euro-Canadians. The somewhat formalized contexts I described earlier often provided the settings for this exchange of information. Both the RCMP officer and the HBC trader at the time were fluent in Inuktitut. The RCMP would receive information about activities in the camps when, as was the custom, camp men visited the detachment while in the settlement. The HBC manager was privy to information through informal conversations held in the store or his home, and by being at the right place at the right time when camp gossip was being passed about within his hearing. Possibly he had better control of information about camp activities because so much of it was passed on to him inadvertently, whereas the discussions held in the police detachment were more susceptible to "information management," or selective transmission. My point, though, is simply that in both settings — the store and the detachment — there were regular opportunities for informational interaction. Also in both settings, however, a certain element of institutionalization was present, in that in fact camp people were rarely invited to visit the Bay manager's residence, or the living quarters attached to the police office. The visits of the Inuit were limited to the formal and bureaucratic settings of the office. The Bay manager had his housekeeper and clerk as sources of information, of course, and police had their special constables, but neither source was immune from engaging in information management. Neither the Bay manager nor the police officer was a regular visitor to the homes of the Mittimatalikmiut, although the police officer took periodic walks through the settlement, at which times he might make brief visits to several Inuit homes.

These patterns of interaction were not the result of discriminatory attitudes on the part of individual managers or officers, but rather had been institutionalized over several decades, and were fairly typical of patterns found in other settlements. Perhaps this formality, entrenched in a new set of traditions, facilitated the Inuit in their dealings with the police and traders, for the structures allowed them to anticipate behaviour. Some of the Tununermiut may have preferred more informality, but my impression was that most were comfortable with the structures. We often appreciate that with which we are familiar, even if it is against our own best interest in the long run. The patterns, of course, are typically colonial.

Turning to the missionaries, we find more informality in relations with the Tununermiut. The Roman Catholic missionary, although he had only one family in his congregation, did not lack for company: Anglicans would regularly visit him. The Catholic priests who worked in the Canadian Arctic usually became fluent in Inuktitut and possessed a high regard for and knowledge of traditional Inuit society and culture. The Catholic missionary in Pond Inlet was probably privy to more of the camp gossip than any other Euro-Canadian. The small residence attached to the mission was rarely empty of Inuit visitors sharing tea and biscuits with the priest, and it did not seem to bother them that he represented a different denominational faith from that to which they had pledged allegiance.

While the Catholic mission was regularly visited by individuals, the Anglican mission was a literal beehive of group activities. The new missionary and his wife made frequent visits to the homes of the Mittimatalikmiut, and both sides seemed to be comfortable with these. The mission residence was almost never empty of visitors, present for formal or informal activities. The resident missionary was extremely concerned with what he considered a rapid rate of secularization among his flock, and he regarded the DNANR as a new impetus to the process. He had determined to try to offset it, by organizing so many church-related activities that parishioners would have little time for the "work of the devil"; and to some extent he succeeded. Church services were held on Sundays and Wednesdays, and during the remainder of the week something was always happening at the mission. There seemed to be a never-ending procession of women walking back and forth to the mission, prayer books in hand, with children clutching the tails of their mothers' parkas or warm inside the inner hoods on their backs. Many activities were organized by the missionary's wife expressly for women, such as Bible study classes and sewing circles. At prayer services women were in attendance but did not vocally participate, as men gave testimonies and prayed for hunting success and good health for their families.

All of the Mittimatalikmiut and any camp people visiting the settlement attended the different functions held at the Anglican mission, but these were not totally successful in combatting the secularization that was of such concern to the missionary. Dances were held regularly in the one-room day school, and although the missionary strongly expressed his disapproval of the events, every-one who attended his services also went to the dances. Over the year of my observations, attendance at mission functions dwindled, as evening activities gradually settled back into a pattern of home visits back and forth. But the mission continued to attract the more devout and perhaps some who were becoming alienated from Inuit life, and church services on Sundays continued to draw full houses.

What I have described in the last few pages was, with the ex-ception of the newly instituted middle-of-the-week meetings at the Anglican mission, the institutionalized pattern of social interaction between Euro-Canadians and Mittimatalikmiut in the settlement during the contact-traditional period. It was within this framework that the DNANR contingent had to carve out a niche for itself, and this context to which it tried to adapt. Initially, both the teachers and the area administrator tried to create a more informal pattern. The administrator and his wife spared no effort to make their home a place that Inuit would feel free to visit at any time of the day or evening. For a while they were successful, as had been the Anglican missionary and his own wife, and several of the older men and women from both the camps and the settlement would drop in to discuss government business with the administrator in his home rather than his office next door. Some simply came by to socialize and share a pot of tea. However, my own impressions were that they often felt uncomfortable in the setting, in spite of their overt impressions of being at ease. Significantly, some of the politically powerful camp men never visited. As that year of change pro-gressed, such visits became less and less frequent. A few stalwarts continued the practice, just as a few men continued to use the sauna, and the open invitation continued to be extended, but in-creasingly the formal visits that prevailed with the police and HBC also prevailed here. Young children would play with the adminis-trator's children and their toys, and some of the younger women in the settlement would help his wife plan Girl Guide activities or other social functions, but even here I noticed that the women seemed to be tense and uncomfortable. The same was true within the homes of the teachers, which in time were almost never visited by Inuit.

With the exception of the administrator and his wife, none of the DNANR Euro-Canadian employees made a regular practice of visiting Mittimatalikmiut homes. The arenas in which they interacted with Inuit were those of the workplace, such as the school or the powerhouse, or extracurricular contexts such as Boy Scout meetings.

Although the mission evening meetings began to drop off in attendance, Inuit individuals and families continued to visit the missionary's home. That he was successful, and the administrator was not, even though he could not speak Inuktitut while the administrator was fluent in it, is attributable to role perceptions. Previous Anglican missionaries may not have been as socially accessible, and perhaps even intrusive, as the new man, but his role had nevertheless been well established by his predecessors, and so it was not difficult for him to modify its characteristics while still working within its traditional and institutionalized structure. The administrator and his colleagues were creating new roles and new role definitions. The administrator, for example, refused to accept the basic characteristics of the well-defined behavioural settings used by the other Euro-Canadian agencies with which the Tununermiut were familiar. He thus, in my opinion, made it difficult for them to accept his new form of interaction. He was, perhaps, breaking too sharply with traditions. The Tununermiut had been exposed in the past to only a small number of Euro-Canadian roles and institutions, and both his behaviour and his position were difficult to fit into the existing structure. Also, of course, he represented a new form of authority, and it was a form of authority about which they were uncertain and confused.

In this chapter I have attempted to delineate the structural features of Tununermiut interactions within the settlement of Pond Inlet during the contact-traditional period, and the structural changes that resulted from the DNANR's appearance on the scene. I have also mentioned some of the ways in which camp people related to the Mittimatalikut. The Tununermiut also maintained relationships with people in other settlements: going back to precontact times, Tununermiut regularly visited Inuit of the Igloolik, Arctic Bay, and Clyde River areas. More recently, people from the Pond Inlet area had been relocated in both Resolute Bay and Grise Fiord. In the case of the former, they had been taken to Resolute to service the Royal Canadian Air Force base and Department of Transport weather station, and in the latter, as mentioned earlier, Tununermiut had been relocated to Grise Fiord to help the Port Harrison evacuees to adapt to hunting conditions in the high Arctic. When possible, letters written in syllabics were sent back and forth between relatives and friends in Pond Inlet and the other two settlements. I was unable to collect demographic data on marriage and other alliances between Tununermiut and the peoples of Igloolik, Arctic Bay, and Clyde River, but my point here is that contacts and ties between the Tununermiut and other Inuit populations existed, and extended back over several centuries. I was struck, ten years after my first visit, when on leaving the settlement of Pond Inlet by aircraft for Resolute Bay, I was accompanied by a young Inuit couple who were on their way to visit relatives in Arctic Bay. However, in spite of these relations with others, the Tununermiut considered themselves to be the "true" Inuit. They were convinced that no other people of the Arctic spoke Inuktitut as well as they did, or, figuratively, stood as tall. Ethnicity and ethnic pride was a reality among the Inuit, and had long been so.

Note

1   I use the male pronoun when referring to NSOs and area administrators because in the 1960s no women were appointed to the position.

A CHANGING POLITICAL PARADIGM,

AND THE IMPACT OF NEW STATUSES

"I can't really recall now what process led me to ask Maktar if
he wanted the job. I knew he was a camp boss, and I knew he was
one of the very best hunters in the area." This excerpt from a letter
from the individual who had been area administrator in Pond Inlet
in 1963–64, a response to a question about his reasons for hiring
Maktar, captures the essentials of political power among the
Tununermiut in contact-traditional times. Maktar had a different
religious affiliation from his fellow Tununermiut — he and his family were Roman Catholic — but he was an excellent hunter and
provider and he held the position of headman. He was a man of
substantial influence and authority, although he had no real power
to force others to accept his decisions. There were others like him,
of his generation, who had similar influence but were not headmen.
Qamaniq, of Aullativik, was one. Because he did not occupy the
position of headman, his authority was not perceived by the administrator and other Euro-Canadians. Had the centralization period not materialized, Qamaniq would have become headman in
time, succeeding his father. Anthropologists who have studied band
societies such as that of the Inuit have long claimed that they are
highly egalitarian. I agree with this to a large extent, but not entirely; in this chapter I will attempt to demonstrate that certain
individuals such as Maktar and Qamaniq directed the lives of others
to a far greater extent than the anthropological literature has recognized, and that their influence was enhanced during the contact-
traditional period.

In traditional times, before contact with the "outside" world
was established, authority was held by the shamans, or *Angakoks*,
and band headmen, or *Isumataqs*. At times the two roles were combined, but typically were discrete from one another. The shaman
probably had more of what we call true power than did the headman, because individuals feared the shaman. Religion was traditionally the major force in Inuit life, and shamans had control over

members of the spirit world — a source of power not available to the headmen, who depended on their own capacities as hunters and secular decision-makers for validation of their right to influence the behaviour of others. A few bad choices on the part of the headman could cause him to lose any influence he might have had, but the shaman's status was not dependent upon such unpredictable factors as, for example, a choice of hunting grounds or the whims of the weather. Also, the shaman could enforce sanctions imposed on individuals who had violated taboos, but the headman had no such power.

It is impossible today to determine the exact intent, but there is little doubt that the role of headman was influenced, and his authority strengthened, through the early contacts with outsiders, or, in the case of the Tununermiut, with Scottish whalers. As happened with many American and Canadian Inuit populations, certain individuals were recognized by the outsiders as spokespersons for their people. It was difficult for Europeans to understand the structure of non-stratified societies. In trading for fresh food, skins, and so on, the Scots who worked the high Arctic waters dealt with individuals who were likely the headmen of the bands, and who became, in a sense, brokers between their own people and the whalers. This offered the possibility of gaining control over relations with the whalers, and access to their trade goods, on which Inuit so quickly became dependent. The position of the headman who played the role of broker, then, was stabilized to a marked degree, and a new dimension was added to the headman's means of status validation. The appointment of Maktar to a position with the DNANR because he was a headman is a recent example of this practice.

Nevertheless, prestige acquired through hunting skills and sound decision-making, as well as demonstration of the traditional value of sharing of meat, continued to form the basis for the influence and authority of headmen. Individual band members were still free to pack their belongings and move to a different band if they lost respect for their headman, and my informants told me that it had not been uncommon to do so. However, the establishment of permanent trading posts, and the tendency towards fairly permanent residence in stable camps located near the posts, must have also enhanced the position of headmen, for individuals had a new commitment to a specific place of residence.

The presence of whalers, then, and later the establishment of a year-round trading post at Pond Inlet, both had effects on the political structure of Tununermiut bands. The most significant event, however, was the arrival of missionaries, and the subsequent conversion of the people to Christianity. It was this that enabled the headman to take on some of the characteristics of shamans, and so to increase their authority substantially. Religion had always been central to the Tununermiut; in earlier chapters I described the high degree of religiosity that characterized them during the contact-traditional period. Living in a material world that was highly unpredictable, the people needed a sense of control over nature, and this, in my opinion, is what religion provided. Obeying the proper taboos was one way of ensuring that the spirits of animals hunted, or the spirits who controlled them, were not offended. The fervour and devotion brought to the traditional animistic and shamanistic religion were transferred to Christianity, and the missionaries, whether they were aware of it or not, were seen as powerful shamans who had personal relationships with the most powerful spirit helper of them all — Jesus Christ. Religious life in the camps was not as structured as that in the settlement, but the intensity of religious feeling demonstrated by camp dwellers was as intense as that of the settlement people.

Most of my observations about Christianity as practised in the camps were made in Aullativik, but I believe that what I saw there was representative of practices in other Tununermiut camps. Twice each Sunday everyone who was not away hunting or visiting the settlement would crowd into Jimmy Muckpah's house for services. Men who were off hunting would hold their own prayer service in a tent or snowhouse, and spend the rest of the day playing cards and drinking tea. The services held in the camp were preceded by prayer meetings that were attended only by men. Each one would recount his sins of the past week and ask for forgiveness and spiritual direction. These monologues were similar to the impassioned testimonials more commonly identified with Pentecostal evangelicism than with Anglicanism. A testimonial might go on for as long as fifteen minutes, with all heads bowed in prayer during it. Anglican theologians tell me the practice is not in fact typically Anglican, but during the year that I observed it, I assumed that it was and so simply took it for granted. Now I wonder whether it may not have been an example of syncretic blending of traditional religious behaviour with elements of Christianity, perhaps with its roots in shamanistic seances. If so, the practice would strengthen my argument about the headman's new role usurping the position of the shaman.

After the men's meeting was concluded, the women and children would join them, each woman bringing with her a prayer book. The services were led by Arniatsiark, the headman, although he would occasionally allow one of the younger men to lead. The service itself was highly formal, with hymn-singing and reading of the liturgy, after which families would return to their own homes for tea and bannock.

It was only in the exercise of his religious leadership that I ever observed Arniatsiark sternly discipline his fellow camp residents. They were members of his camp but were also, in a sense, his "flock," and he felt responsible for their spiritual well-being. On one occasion, for example, he became quite concerned because he felt that the rate of absenteeism from Sunday morning services had reached alarming proportions. He went to each house in the camp and informed the men that in the future they were to attend services every week or else leave Aullativik. I can only guess at how he would have followed through on his threat to banish backsliders, for the next Sunday everyone attended both services, and continued to do so for several more weeks.

In my view, the above observations coalesce in the claim that the role of the headman, after the introduction of Christianity, was blended with that of shaman. In his role as lay minister in the camp, the headman had taken on a new basis for the exercise of authority, based on the perceived ability to call upon the spirit of Jesus Christ, rather than traditional spirit helpers as had been the case with the shamans. Also, unlike the Tununermiut's relations with other contact agencies, those the headman had with the mission gave him almost complete autonomy of action. He interpreted Christianity for his own people in their own terms. This was in some ways merely an artifact of living in the isolated camps, of course, beyond the constant scrutiny of the resident missionary. However, the Anglican church has a history in the Canadian Arctic of trying, more than any other contact agency, to turn its work over to the Inuit themselves for control and goal definition. It is no surprise, therefore, that it has been more successful in achieving the aim to which all agencies have given lip service: to work themselves out of their jobs; to be replaced by Inuit. As I write this, there is an active rumour in Anglican church circles about the likely appointment of an Inuk as the next Bishop of the Arctic.

Unfortunately, I do not know to what extent the headmen *qua* lay missionaries actively sought to displace the traditional shaman. Whether they thought of their new position as a means of acquiring power or not, in fact exactly that occurred, with the consequence that the power relationships in the camps were dramatically changed. I also do not know whether the missionaries actively promoted the process, seeing it as a way to rid themselves of the problem of shamans, or if they were even aware of it.

In spite of the changes in the power base of headmen brought about by the contact-traditional period, individual prestige in the camps was still acquired through demonstration of the traditional virtues, such as effective decision-making, hunting skill, and sharing of food. But a new basis on which prestige could be acquired came about as a result of the contact-traditional period, and I think its development is of crucial importance in understanding later political events among the Tununermiut and other Inuit of the Canadian Arctic.

At the end of the last chapter, speaking of the Tununermiut's relationship with other Inuit populations, I referred to their "ethnic" status. This use of "ethnic" is admittedly a somewhat popularized one (which still, I believe, meets the basic criteria of most anthropological definitions); "ethnicity" more strictly refers to a population with a sense of its own distinct identity, existing within a larger social environment that surrounds and to a considerable extent dominates it, at least economically. In that sense, the Tununermiut were truly an ethnic population during the contact-traditional period — involved as they were within the larger context of Canadian society — and they would become even more so during the centralization period that followed.

A major characteristic of ethnicity is an attempt on the part of the ethnic population to retain, and perhaps portray to the larger society, its continuing distinctiveness. Members engage in what Gerald Berreman has called "impression-management" (Berreman, 1962). This involves the adoption of specific postures towards both members of their own group and members of the larger society. For the Tununermiut this meant, during the contact-traditional period, the displaying of what might be termed an "Inuit-orientation." That is, individuals, and particularly ones who had worked for one of the contact agencies in the settlement, would self-consciously demonstrate that they were still true Inuit in the fullest sense. Perhaps the point was to demonstrate that they had not been contaminated by association with outsiders and wage employment. In any event, when everyone you know is Inuit, there is no need to make an issue of your Inuit identity, although trying to manifest valued Inuit behaviour, such as success at hunting, would be an advantage in acquiring prestige. In the new context of ethnicity, however, it became important to show that one was *still* an Inuit, and the capacity to do so became in its right a means of acquiring prestige. There were several strategies employed to do this.

Perhaps the example of Qamaniq, the son of Arniatsiark, who was headman in Aullativik, will best illustrate one such strategy. If the period of centralization had not occurred, ringing the knell for camp life, Qamaniq would likely have assumed his father's position in time. To do so, however, he would also have had to delicately balance different aspects of his life-style. He was very much an innovator, as I have suggested earlier, and in time was to become an entrepreneur. There is no question that he was influenced by and appreciative of many aspects of Euro-Canadian life. Qamaniq was for quite a while the only man in Aullativik who owned a high-powered .222 rifle with a telescopic scope; he wore an expensive "Siwash" sweater, which made him look more like a Northwest Coast Indian than an Inuk; and he had made beds for his family, preferring them to the traditional sleeping platform. He even created his own radio station for his camp. He was adept at repairing watches and clocks, and did repair work for many of the Tununermiut in the area. Was he, then, basically oriented towards the outside world, which continued to encroach upon the Tununermiut? I believe that he was essentially a pragmatist, and when it suited him he was more than prepared to selectively adopt material items from that world. He was also, and consciously so, a headman in the making. He demonstrated the traditional virtues in elegant fashion. When he hunted with other men, it was Qamaniq who made the telling decisions, and he was an excellent hunter. (Of course, his rifle gave him a distinct advantage over the other men, who used the bulky Lee-Enfield .303s.) Qamaniq's reputation extended far beyond Aullativik; he was highly respected by men in other camps.

How, then, did Qamaniq walk the tight-rope between the two cultures? He did so by accepting the material benefits of the contact situation while refusing to become too involved in the social world of the outsiders. He practised social avoidance in his dealings with Euro-Canadians, and he urged others to do so as well. When Jimmy Muckpah accepted a job with the HBC in Pond Inlet, Qamaniq urged him to quit, which Jimmy did. I recall many occasions when Euro-Canadians in the settlement would make reference to Qamaniq in puzzled terms. He was an enigma to them. Most considered him to be a quiet, somewhat withdrawn individual who, when in the settlement, would conduct his business and then return home as quickly as possible. To them, he was not the dynamic and strong-willed personality that he was among the Tununermiut, and he was certainly not considered a leader.

Qamaniq's avoidance of extended Euro-Canadian contacts was,

I am convinced, the result of a conscious effort on his part to maintain his status within Tununermiut society: a status predicated in traditional terms, but also modified because of the realities of the contact situation. That is, his posture enabled him, or so he hoped, to perpetuate in his own person and to demonstrate to others the autonomous and vital life-style that was the Inuit way. It enabled him to maintain status while also taking from the contact situation those things he desired.

There are many examples of the problems individuals had in maintaining Inuit-orientation while also working for contact agencies. The person who perhaps had most difficulty doing this was the previously mentioned Danielee, who had the best-paying job of any of the Tununermiut. He spent a large portion of his salary on foodstuffs so that he could provide traditional hospitality to camp people visiting the settlement, but my impression was that he had virtually abandoned hope of retaining any high status among the Tununermiut. In a sense, despite his economic efforts, he had stepped over the thin line between the two societies; but his situation was extreme. Others chose to leave agency employment and return to the land: it was necessary for them to revalidate themselves and their Inuit-orientation.

One former wage worker was Kudluk, who was headman in Illukisaat, the only camp at that time situated on Bylot Island. Although Kudluk had worked for the RCMP as a special constable some years earlier, he was a highly influential person in terms of the rather amorphous camp political system, and a man of considerable prestige. His house was sparsely furnished: here there were no beds or expensive radios, but rather, simple austerity. There was no evidence of the material benefits of his earlier work with the RCMP.

Although his camp was relatively close to the settlement, Kudluk made only infrequent visits to it, and those for specific purposes such as trading or visiting the Anglican mission. He was considered by both Tununermiut and Euro-Canadians to be an excellent hunter and a man of quiet dignity, whose camp, although small, was well maintained. He was characteristic of several older men living in the camps who had had experience working for contact agencies in the past, and had then rejected these backgrounds in order to reaffirm their Inuit-orientation. They seemed to consciously repudiate any acculturative influences other than their religious conversion to Christianity.

Some of these individuals had, like Kudluk, become camp headmen. These found the two new sources of prestige and therefore influence available to them: demonstration of an Inuit-orientation and the role of lay minister. In some respects they became role models for younger men such as Qamaniq, who also sought to emphasize their Inuit identity, but the latter, because they had not been tainted by close association with Euro-Canadians, could be more openly accepting of the material benefits offered by the outside world. Both generations who adopted the stance of Inuit-orientation seemed to me to be attempting to create a new Inuit political reality that was continuous with the past but also filled the apparent power vacuum in which the increasing number of Inuit who worked for Euro-Canadian agencies found themselves. This was to become very important when the Tununermiut discovered in the centralization period that their traditional way of life was rapidly eroding. Inuit-orientation became a mechanism for perpetuating, if not a way of life, at least a sense of continuity.

The Emergence of a New Generation of Leaders

Three young men were emerging as leaders in the period just prior to centralization, when the Tununermiut moved en masse into the settlement. One of them was Qamaniq, whom we have already discussed. He had taken one extreme position, which was to emphasize his Inuit-orientation by refusing to enter the social realm of the Euro-Canadians, and he maintained this position even after the centralization period occurred and he found wage employment in Pond Inlet.

Kaunak, the son of Kudluk of Illukisaat, whom we met earlier, was a second. The son of a camp headman who had once worked for the RCMP, Kaunak was also married to the daughter of a former special constable, Joe Panikpakutasak, who had been unable to return to the land after retirement because of poor health. His sister-in-law was one of the few Tununermiut to have made a complete break with her people by working for a while as an airline stewardess before taking up residence in Montreal. Kaunak himself had been hired by the area administrator and was being trained for the position of special assistant, when he passed away quite suddenly. Kaunak bridged the two worlds in which he lived successfully, although perhaps somewhat precariously. In his demeanour he demonstrated an Inuit-orientation: his home in the settlement was simply furnished, and he maintained a dog team and hunted whenever he had free time. While Danielee, who also worked for the DNANR, had, like Qamaniq, embraced the material benefits of wage labour, Kaunak led an austere life. There is of course no way of knowing how, had he lived, he might have maintained his position and developed a power base in the changing political vortex.

When Kaunak died, the area administrator replaced him with Maktar, a member of the only Roman Catholic family among the Tununermiut of the time, and one of the best hunters in the area. His religious affiliation seems not to have hurt his political position, for he was headman in his own camp at the time he was hired. Most of the residents of that camp were close relatives of his, though, and also Catholic. Nevertheless, he was highly regarded by all of the Tununermiut men. I believe that he accepted the position because it would allow him to live near the Roman Catholic mission, and in fact he sought consent of the resident priest before he did so. It was my impression that he also had political objectives in mind.

Maktar had earned his credentials as an Inuit-oriented camp leader and had established himself within the traditional political structure. At the same time, he seemed to be cognizant of the developments occurring in the settlement and was able to forecast the demise of camp life and the exodus of camp people to Pond Inlet. He wanted to have some influence on future developments and directions, and the best place to do that was the settlement itself. Like Kaunak, Maktar maintained a demeanour of traditionality while also working full-time for the DNANR. He had a firm position in the Inuit structure, and was to create a position for himself in the structure to come. During the centralization period, for example, when elections to community councils were called, Maktar would be in a position to run for office, and to do so successfully.

There were at that time, then, two separate and yet related political processes occurring among the Tununermiut. On the one hand, there were the developments on the land, which were beginning to look like the basis for an incipient revitalization movement within the contact-traditional values. Those adopting this stance expressed it in part by actively avoiding close identification with Euro-Canadian society. I do not believe that this movement was recognized by many of the Euro-Canadians, who often made the hoary colonialistic mistake of assuming that individuals who made social overtones to them were also individuals who had high prestige in the traditional context. They were victims of a sophisticated form of impression-management.

Not all camp people accepted this quasi-revitalization orientation, but while still living in the camps they were to a great extent under the influence if not authority of their headmen and others like Qamaniq who were decision-makers. I do not wish to imply that these "leaders" were consciously conspiring against Euro-Canadian influences or in any respect saw themselves as constituting a united front. Indeed, as was the case with Qamaniq and Maktar, there was often a subtle form of competition between them. There was in the camps, then, a basis for factionalism, but more cogently, an incipient ideological cohesion and increasing support for the incipient movement. The underlying political system of the Tununermiut, which had been ignored by most outside observers, was being brought out and objectified, in my opinion. At that time I predicted the growth of a true revitalization movement on the land, and the emergence of an ethos which was more "traditional" than "contact" in nature. It did occur in many respects, but in the settlement rather than the camps. It emerged several years later, and its goals were more clearly in accord with those of other minority peoples struggling for self-determination than they were with the perpetuation of a traditional way of life.

The second process, or perhaps direction is a better term, was similar in many respects to what Vallee (1962) characterized for Baker Lake as the orientation of the Kabloonamiut. The individuals and families who adopted this orientation, and so fostered this process, according to Vallee were those who because of type of employment, personal characteristics, or simply personal preferences had formed and nurtured affiliations with Euro-Canadians. There were some Kabloonamiut in the camps and the settlement of Pond Inlet in the early 1960s. Not all worked for Euro-Canadian agencies, and certainly some, who had such employment, were not of this type. However, there was definitely a correlation between wage employment and the adoption of a Kabloonamiut stance.

In the settlement the Kabloonamiut, if I may continue to borrow Vallee's term, were individuals who had adopted the stance not so much out of preference as out of necessity. They included the two RCMP special constables; a widow who worked as a housekeeper in the home of the area administrator; the retired special constable, Joe Panikpakutsak; and a few others. Most of these had had the posture thrust upon them by virtue of their jobs, or their inability to engage in traditional activities. For those who had jobs, the nature of the work required close interaction with Euro-Canadians, and it was felt necessary to display the demeaning behavioural traits that native employees have so often had to assume in colonial situations. Their employers may not have required such behaviour, but the subservient nature of the employment seemed to the incumbents to demand it. These individuals usually had lost status within the Inuit population. Camp people often ridiculed them behind their backs and considered them to have lost one of the most prized qualities of Inuit life — independence. Being socially segregated from the Inuit communities, they were increasingly forced to turn to Euro-Canadians for social gratification. They might attempt to create new behavioural settings in which they could interact with Euro-Canadians by, for example, developing visiting patterns with Euro-Canadians such as the teachers, who could not speak Inuktitut. There were also some elderly individuals living in the camps who seemed to enjoy being with the Euro-Canadians and visiting them in their homes. Such persons were past the stage of life where prestige is important, and besides, they had achieved a high enough status through long lives of living on the hand that they were not threatened or stigmatized by this behaviour.

Some of the Kabloonamiut, then, would consciously seek out situations in which they would be forced to use the little English skills they possessed. This was in complete contradiction to the linguistic behaviour of those who had adopted an Inuit-orientation. All of the Tununermiut who lived in the settlement had some facility in English, however minimal, and in fact this was a necessity for those who worked for the DNANR, for only the area administrator could speak Inuktitut. Many of the camp people also had some ability to speak English. However, almost all refused to use their English skills verbally. I believe that this was a deliberate posture, not taken out of some sense of embarrassment over their inadequacies to grasp the language. I recall several times when women who had worked for Euro-Canadian agencies sat listening attentively to English conversations and then looked up quizzically when asked a question in that language. It may be that this disavowal of English was their way of demonstrating an Inuit-orientation and showing that they had not been converted to the Euro-Canadian ways, even though they had worked in the settlement. However, this manipulation of language was to become a major means of retaining Inuit identity on a personal level and cohesion on a societal one in the soon-to-be-experienced centralization period.

I may have belaboured this discussion of different political currents running through Tununermiut society near the end of the contact-traditional period, and I have to admit that the typologies and categories I have presented were not as clearcut as I may seem to be suggesting. Nevertheless, changes in political behaviour were occurring among the people, and like other changes they had experienced in recent times, these were responses to alien influences.

The revitalization movement I have tried to describe was not a "return to the land" movement, for most of the people still lived in camps. The fact that they did move into the settlements less than five years after the time I am describing here may suggest that the movement was never much of a reality in any sense. I would disagree; there was a new and objectified conception of Inuit identity being formed, and it would be carried along with the camp people as they moved into Pond Inlet, took up wage employment, and accepted governmental housing, formal instruction for their children, new foods, and all the rest of the paraphernalia that were part of the centralization period.

The revitalization movement was of an intellectual nature, and the seeds planted during its formative stages would blossom into a sense of Inuit consciousness that would carry the Tununermiut through a period of change more dramatic than any they had yet faced. The movement was not so much characterized by the idea of "let us return to" as one of "let us hold on to." What was forged during the contact-traditional period, then, would in my opinion shape many developments during the centralization period.

THE SETTLEMENT TEN YEARS LATER

During the decade that elapsed between my two field trips to Pond Inlet, I temporarily shifted my interests to study the development of single-industry towns in northern Canada, but I also conducted research with the Inuit populations of Rankin Inlet and Yellowknife in the Northwest Territories. Several Tununermiut had taken up government positions in Ottawa, working on language projects, and I maintained close contact with them during the intervening period, as well as keeping up correspondence with people in the settlement of Pond Inlet itself. I had been prepared, then, to encounter changes, and I had some idea of the effects of the termination of camp life on the Tununermiut, but my first day back in the settlement brought me more surprises than I could possibly have anticipated.

Once again, I arrived without any previous notice being given to residents. I should have written ahead, but had neglected to do so. On this trip I did not have to arrange for a charter from Resolute Bay, because there were regularly scheduled flights between it and Pond Inlet. The aircraft was piloted by a young Inuk, and there were several passengers besides myself. These were Inuit returning from visits to the south and government scientists and bureaucrats. When we arrived in Pond Inlet, instead of landing on the grassy plain behind the settlement, the aircraft set down on a newly constructed airstrip at the end of which was a small terminal.

Even though incoming aircraft were no longer a novelty, and mail was delivered on a regular basis, it seemed that the entire community turned out to meet us. People were curious to see who might be on the plane and eager for an opportunity to break the monotony of a long summer evening. At first, as I looked over the crowd, I recognized no one, but then I spotted a familiar face. I walked over to my old friend Qamaniq, who stood beside his wife, and extended my hand in greeting. I did not expect the startled look on his face when I did so, but his amazement turned out to be understandable: he had heard a rumour that I had died. I have never been sure whether he thought he was seeing a ghost, or whether he was simply taken aback at seeing someone who looked so much like me. His wife, Koonoo, was first to recognize me. We shook hands and tried to carry on a brief conversation. Qamaniq did not have to use the technique of impression-management to avoid speaking English, for he had never felt moved to learn it; and I had forgotten most of my Inuktitut. But we were able to communicate in a stumbling fashion, and I asked him for directions to the transient centre, where I was to stay. He surprised me by offering me a ride in his automobile. I gratefully accepted. In the same day I was to be both flown in an aircraft, and driven in a car, by Inuit men — a striking difference from the days of dogteams.

Koonoo, who was dressed in a fashionable vinyl jacket, took the children who were with them home, and Qamaniq drove me to the centre. Several days of heavy rains had turned the steep road down the hill from the landing strip to the settlement into a thick, oozy gumbo. As the small black Fiat slithered from side to side, I wondered briefly whether I had been wise in accepting the ride, but Qamaniq handled the car with skill and aplomb, and we soon arrived safely at the transient centre. Before leaving, Qamaniq invited me to visit his home that afternoon after work, giving me the street name and number of his address, and telling me to phone him if I had trouble finding it. I had experienced the first of many shocks I would receive during the next few days. My friend Qamaniq, the hunter and man of the land, now lived in Pond Inlet in a house that had a street number and a telephone, worked at full-time wage employment that had regular hours, and owned his own car. I later learned that he used his car as a taxi, transporting visitors from the airstrip to the transient centre.

The following day I walked slowly through the greatly expanded settlement, meeting old friends and acquaintances along the way, and trying to absorb the many visual changes. The rocky, tundra-covered hill beyond the stream that had earlier marked the edge of the settlement was now covered with small homes, a school, a large nursing station, and sundry other buildings. This was the DNANR section of the community, which had begun to take some sort of ragged shape ten years before. At the other end, the "old" settlement was but little changed. Father Rousseliere still lived in the small quarters attached to his mission church. The HBC residence and the RCMP detachment still stood close to one another, surrounded by neatly manicured grass that was lushly green after the rains of the past few days. (This same rain had turned the DNANR area, which was not landscaped, into a huge mud puddle.) The HBC store had been expanded, and the Anglican mission now

A new section of Pond Inlet. 1973.

had its own church building, but in spite of these changes I felt that I had stepped back in time as I walked through this part of the settlement.

That afternoon I began the walk up the hill to Qamaniq's house, but on the way I was stopped by a handsome young man with long, black hair and modish sunglasses. He asked me in virtually unaccented English if I was on my way to Qamaniq's house, and if so, would I like a ride there. I was quick to accept, for the hill was steep and I was out of condition. I had not noticed the car parked alongside the path, but we climbed into it and drove the rest of the way. Not until I entered the house and was introduced to him did I realize that the young man was Timothy, Qamaniq's oldest son, who had been a six-year-old child when I last saw him. My mind flitted back to the Aullativik of a decade before, and to the image of a small boy posing for a picture in front of his father's house and holding in his arms his two favourite toys, a seal embryo that his father had cut from the stomach of an animal he had killed, and a skinned carcass of a fox. Both had taken some time to rot, for each night he would leave them in the outer snowhouse attached to his father's dwelling, where they would freeze as hard as rock, to be played with again the following day. Timothy acted as my interpreter during my visit that evening, and before I had been there long he told me that his father wished me to stay for dinner. After having accepted, I was offered a whiskey and water before the meal. We then shared a delicious meal of fried arctic char, a delicacy I had not enjoyed for several years. Instead of cooking it over a soapstone *kudlik*, Qamaniq's wife used her fairly modern stove. Speaking through Timothy, she apologized for not serving vegetables with the fish, explaining that the HBC was very low on supplies while the manager awaited sealift.

The three-bedroom bungalow stood on the crest of the high hill that swept across the back of the settlement, at the end of a long, crescent-shaped street, and overlooked a large, grassy expanse youngsters used as a playing field. In the distance was a stunning view across Eclipse Sound of Bylot Island with its high peaks and glaciers. I could not help thinking to myself, "Leave it to Qamaniq to get the best location in the settlement for his own home!" His father, Arniatsiark, who had been headman in Aullativik, lived next door, and beside Arniatsiark was the home of Kadloo, who had also lived in Aullativik in 1963. The close proximity of these three residences did not mean, I later discovered, that camp people had formed their own little communities when they moved into the settlement, but there had been some tendency to select residences close to families from the same camps. Qamaniq's younger brother, Samuellee, who had lived in Aullativik the year before I spent my time there, lived at some distance from Qamaniq and their father. His wife was postmistress, however, and that may have influenced his choice of location.

During dinner that evening, Qamaniq asked me if I would like to stay with him and his family while I was in the settlement. I was worried because, although his house was far more spacious than the one in which I had lived with him in Aullativik a decade before, we had all aged ten years in the interim; it might be difficult for his wife to put up with an outsider, and, possibly more importantly, with five children ranging in ages from four to sixteen living in the same house, I was sure I would be an inconvenience to all concerned. I told him that while I appreciated the offer and would very much like to move in, I would think on the idea for a day.

The transient centre was crowded with visiting scientists, a Bell telephone crew and their pilots, an auditor from the Territorial government who had arrived on the same plane as I, a team of scuba divers from Yellowknife who were interested in finding narwhal skeletons, and a geographer from Germany. The HBC store was out of food, and the manager was eagerly anticipating sealift and, with it, new supplies. The crews and most of the scientists had their own food reserves and were eating well. I had a supply of freeze-dried foods that I had brought with me for emergency use, but I doubted that they would last for several weeks. A construction crew was to arrive at any time to begin work on a new school, and so conditions in the transient centre were, although comfortable enough, less than perfect. The evening spent with Qamaniq and his family had reminded me of the warmth and sense of intimacy that one experiences in an Inuit home. Possibly, Canadian rural family life before family sizes began to dwindle had a similar intimacy but without, I would think, the constant visiting back and forth, day and night, that characterizes and has traditionally characterized Inuit home life. After some thought, therefore, I decided to accept Qamaniq's invitation, and the following day he picked up my bags and drove me to his house. I was properly embarrassed when I realized that I was to be given a room of my own, and the children would be made to sleep in the larger room together, as ten years before I had been accorded no such amenities; but the die was cast and I did not regret it. I hope they did not either. There was no arguing with Qamaniq.

Many of the things I will say about the community as I found it that second time will have to be superficial and rather impressionistic, for I wasn't there long enough to gain the depth I had hoped for, and also, much of my time was spent working with files and records of community associations, which had to be done in the government office building. However, I do believe that, because of the relationship I was fortunate enough to develop with the Tununermiut ten years before, I still had some rapport. Older people would stop me on the street or in the HBC store and ask if I was not the person who had lived with Jimmy Muckpah at Aullativik. It was good to be remembered. And, living with Qamaniq, I was daily in the centre of one of the main arenas of interaction in the settlement. For both of these reasons, I had free access to most homes in the settlement. Because of the food shortage, I once again adapted to "land food," or seal, caribou, and fish, for these were the only foods available to the people.

A Home in the Settlement

A short tour through Qamaniq's home will illustrate some of the material changes the Tununermiut had experienced. The front door, which faced out onto the settlement below, was not used as an entrance, as it was several feet above ground level and no connecting stairs had been built. One entered by the side door. Outside that door, on the small porch, stood a freezer filled with arctic char and caribou meat. A small entry hall opened on the left into the combined kitchen/living room and on the right to a small storage room. The main room faced out on one side, over the settlement, and the bedrooms were at the opposite end of it from the entry hall. The bathroom separated the master bedroom from the other two.

Rifles, clothing, and odds and ends were kept in the storeroom. On entering, people would usually remove their shoes or boots and leave them in the entry hall. The bathroom had a sink and a toilet but no running water. Discarded water ran down the drain and under the house where it spilled onto the ground. The "honey bag" toilet had an air vent on the back. There was a large mirror above the sink, and on the wall across the room were protruding shelves covered with shaving equipment and assorted toiletries. A wringer washing machine stood in a corner and was brought into the kitchen area when washing needed to be done. A short hallway ran from the bathroom to the main room, and on one side of it was the furnace.

The kitchen/living room was dominated by a table, placed squarely in its middle, and four kitchen chairs. The day after I moved into her home, Koonoo cut out and attached new plastic covers for the chairs, which accentuated the family's recently adopted concern with Euro-Canadian expressions of hospitality and caused me further embarrassment. A large, black, oil-burning stove stood along the outside wall, and there was always a huge three- or four-gallon container of water sitting on the rear of it. Whenever water was taken for washing, it was immediately replaced. Two full porcelain teapots were ever-present on one side of the stove, and anyone who desired could help themselves at any time. (In contact-traditional times loose tea was used, and the tea kettle, which also served as the tea pot, was rarely emptied. White leaves would continually filter into the cups along with the hot liquid. In 1974 tea bags were used. Ten years before they would have been an unattainable luxury on all but special occasions.) In the corner by the outside door stood the water tank, and beside it the modern refrigerator. Next to the refrigerator was the large kitchen sink, and above the sink, on both sides of the corner, were high cupboards. Along the wall beside the sink was an arborite-covered counter with extra cupboards and drawers below. Sitting on the counter most of the time were an electric kettle and electric frying pan. The cupboards were well stocked with tableware, pots, and pans and the drawers with silverware and carving utensils. In one cupboard, salt, pepper, and assorted spices were kept. Bright new canisters stood on the counter beside the electric kettle. One of the cupboards was filled with twelve bread pans. Koonoo made excellent raised bread, which she sold to Euro-Canadian families in the settlement. Although the younger children preferred this lighter bread, she still made bannock for Qamaniq and herself.

At the other end of the room was a chesterfield that was regularly covered with children's jackets, comic books, and toys. Across from the chesterfield was a matching chair, and behind the chair a closet used for outer garments. A high bookcase stood beside this chair and was filled to overflowing with knick-knacks, souvenirs, and neatly stacked piles of outdoor magazines and mail order catalogues. Sporting goods catalogues were kept in a separate pile from the department store ones, and both were kept separate from service manuals and automotive catalogues. A few books were scattered among the piles, and two first-aid kits were kept on the lower shelf. On the top shelf stood a short-wave band radio that was used each afternoon and evening to listen to the local Inuktitut-language radio station, with a cassette tape recorder beside it. Next to these were the alarm clock, which, I found, rang its alarm at unpredictable times, and several boxes of cassette tapes. On the walls of the room hung a cuckoo clock, two calendars, a barometer, religious plaques, and posters advertising scenic places of interest in Montreal, which Qamaniq and Koonoo had visited twice. Beneath the window that looked out over the settlement stood a small telephone stand, and on top of it perched the most heavily used item in the room — the telephone.

In one of the children's bedrooms there was a set of metal bunk beds, and in the other a heavy wooden set made by Qamaniq. The day I moved in with his family, and while I was out of the house, he sawed the latter in half, moved the resulting two beds into the larger of the children's rooms, and put the metal bunk beds into the smaller one where I was to sleep. I used the upper one as a storage place. Both sets of beds had new, very comfortable mattresses. There was a chest of drawers in each of these rooms, and two in the master bedroom. Each bedroom had a closet, which was used to store suitcases and other items as well as clothing. The master bedroom had a large double bed.

The appearance of Qamaniq's home in Pond Inlet in 1974, with its many and varied furnishings, would lead one to believe that his life-style had changed dramatically since he left his residence in Aullativik; and indeed it had. Activities within the home were no longer characterized by the randomness and freedom that had typified life in a camp dwelling, but were instead regulated by the clock. Older males of post-school age had to keep regular working hours, and small children had to be up in the mornings to prepare for school. The traditional use of time during the summer months, when the circling midnight sun allowed continuous outdoor activity, was retained to some degree, although within the new structures it almost became a burden for individuals to do so. Women would stay up all night, for example, and then send their children off to school before retiring themselves in the morning hours. Men might spend all night drinking coffee and socializing with one another, as they would have done a decade before while planning a hunt, but then they would have to prepare for work in the morning. Qamaniq, who was now a heavy equipment operator, told me on one occasion that he failed to understand why he could not do his allotted work and put in his eight hours after midnight. He had been unsuccessful in convincing his Euro-Canadian foreman of the validity of his argument, even though he was fully prepared to do just as good a job, and at hours that would allow for more time to interact with his friends.

Even with these changes, however, the aura of sociability that had permeated homes in the camps was still very apparent in Qamaniq's home in the settlement. The telephone, which permitted an extension of it, by linking the home with others, was rarely idle.

Qamaniq, whom I had thought destined to become a headman, had truly gone through many changes since I had last seen him. Shortly after I left Pond Inlet in 1964, he was selected to go to British Columbia for several months of training as a heavy equipment operator. At the time, he had been considering following the mass migration of the Tununermiut to Pond Inlet, and while he was away on training his family made the move to the settlement. Before returning home, he spent several months working as an apprentice in Frobisher Bay. It seems that his entire orientation to life had been modified by these experiences, but more likely the apparent changes in style were merely variations on the theme of his existing personality and motivations. Always a pragmatist, he had seen the inevitability of the major residential and economic changes that were to be part of centralization, and decided to maximize his own position within the newly emerging system. His Inuit orientation did not change, in spite of overt appearances. In the settlement he interacted only with other Inuit, except in work-related situations. During the several weeks I lived with his family, not a single other Euro-Canadian entered the home. Young Inuit visiting his children were usually startled to find me there, for my

Formerly a source of fresh water for Pond Inlet. 1973.

presence was the breaking of a visiting pattern. (I was flattered, of course, to have been made an exception.)

For nine years, Qamaniq had worked with the local Department of Public Works (DPW) in Pond Inlet. A short while before I returned to the settlement, he had taken his wife and oldest son on a trip to Montreal. The son had gone along as interpreter for his still virtually monolingual parents. The DPW in Pond Inlet was under the jurisdiction of the territorial government, and as an employee, Qamaniq was eligible for such trips to the south at government expense, just as were Euro-Canadians, who would use them to visit relatives. He had taken a trip to Montreal once before, and while he told me that he had found it too warm, he had enjoyed the adventure. On this second journey, he visited a Fiat dealer and, having earlier purchased a Fiat automobile that had been shipped north by boat, he bought himself a professional parts catalogue. This would enable him to order replacements for any broken or worn-out parts that he was not able to repair himself. It is interesting that the only other automobile in Pond Inlet in 1974 was a Volkswagen that had been abandoned by its Euro-Canadian owner because he was unable to maintain it. Qamaniq's vehicle was always in running order, unless he was awaiting a shipment of parts. That same year he won the local shooting competition, demonstrating that he retained the skills he had honed during his hunting days, and he had then gone to Frobisher Bay for the regional competition.

I did wonder that first evening, as I shared a drink and dinner with Qamaniq in his settlement home, whether he had also changed as an individual. His house was typical of others in the settlement, and I thought of other Tununermiut sitting down for meals in their houses that same evening, wondering how they had fared during the past decade and whether they had made the transition as well as Qamaniq and his family seemed to have done.

That same evening I went to the house next door to pay my respects to Arniatsiark, Qamaniq's father and headman in Aullativik a decade earlier. I brought with me some snapshots of camplife and of Arniatsiark's children when they were younger. The elderly leader, who was employed as a house painter in the settlement, seemed at first not to recognize the scenes and the individuals in them. His wife identified them for him, and then took pleasure in the images of an earlier time, but I also sensed an attitude of fatalism as he perused them, as if he had long before accepted that the life of the camps, and of hunters, was only a set of memories. His oldest son, who was home on leave from a job on an oil rig on one of the more northerly islands, told me during my visit of his own life. Whenever he was home, he said, he would take his rifle and go out on the land to hunt. When I last saw him, he was a youth who was being initiated into the role of hunter by his uncle Qamaniq. He had been proud of his new status, and now, ten years later, was holding on to it in his own way. Later in the evening I returned to Qamaniq's home, and after a cup of tea and a slice of homemade bread fell asleep to dream of my newly reclaimed friends in their previous life.

I had returned to Pond Inlet to study the evolution of political and quasi-political structures that had followed the formation of a Settlement Council in 1965. Convinced as I was that there had been more politically motivated behaviour among the traditional Tununermiut than the generalized anthropological image of Inuit would admit, I expected that political skills would be employed in the new structures in the settlement, perhaps in innovative ways. (To anticipate a later discussion: my hypothesis seems to have been proven correct.)

The Council was one of several organizations formed, the others being the Toonoonik-Sahoonik Co-operative, the Hunters and Trappers Association, and the Housing Association. Since its inception, the Council had been under the ultimate authority of the settlement manager (a new title for the position of area administrator), and in its formative years had been regarded by Euro-Canadians in the settlement as a token and powerless organization. The perception had some validity, for ultimately all decisions had to be ratified by the manager, who in turn had to seek approval from his own superiors in Frobisher Bay, Ottawa, or Yellowknife. To anticipate, however, its members, most of whom were Inuit, were struggling to create a more autonomous base for their activities, whether decision-making or implementation of decisions.

What were the events leading to these enormous changes that completely transformed the lives of the Tununermiut and other Inuit across the Canadian Arctic, in the 1960s and 1970s? The experience of Arniatsiark's oldest son was not unusual among his peers, for many of the youth of Pond Inlet had found employment with Pan-Arctic, an oil exploration company, and worked on rigs several hundred miles north of their homes. After working on the sites for twenty days, they would be flown home for ten days of rest and recuperation and then transported back to the rig. If they were not living in the atomic age, these sons of hunters were at least firmly entrenched in the "jet age," and seemed by and large to have adapted to the transition effectively. Some of the young men unfortunately came into contact with soft drugs such as marijuana while working on rigs, and a few returned home with drugs and introduced their younger siblings to them; but in general they seemed to me to be handling their modified life-style well.

A few days after I had taken up residence in Qamaniq's home, I talked with a young Inuk from Arctic Bay who was passing through Pond Inlet on his way home to relax after his stint on the rigs. He was both articulate and bitter. When I asked him about the movement into the settlements from the camps, he claimed that the people had been forced to move by governmental pressure. He was convinced that the older people, and camp headmen in particular, had been told that unless they moved to the settlement many economic benefits they enjoyed, such as family allowances and old age pensions, would no longer be available to them. I had done previous research in settings where aboriginal peoples had been forced to relocate by subtle use of governmental pressure combined with residents' lack of understanding of their rights to refuse the move; and so I was tempted to accept this explanation. I no longer think that the impetus for centralization was for the Tununermiut quite as contrived as I believed that evening, but I do think that the Tununermiut who accepted centralization did so without full understanding of the implications. Certainly, the relocation was fostered by representatives of the governments of Canada and the Northwest Territories.

One major factor leading to centralization was the home-building program. Before I left the area in 1964 a few prefabricated houses had been built in camps, but primarily in those nearest to the settlement. Shortly after, however, new Inuit housing was only made available in Pond Inlet itself. (I have only my Inuit informants' word for this, as I was unable to obtain any government information on housing policies of the time.) People desired the better housing and in many cases were prepared to move to Pond Inlet for it. With the acquisition of snowmobiles, men could live in the settlement and still continue to hunt over large territories. Most expected to continue the contact-traditional way of life while living in the settlements.

A second factor was the increasing enrolment of children in the federal day school in Pond Inlet. Parents did not entirely approve of having their children live for months each year in government-managed hostels, yet they were unable to keep them out of school (for economic reasons: to do so would have meant forfeiting their family allowance cheques). A move into the settlement meant that families who had children in school would not be disrupted, as the school-aged children could live at home.

Jobs became increasingly available in the settlement as the DNANR operations grew, and with them, the Euro-Canadian personnel required to manage them. Inuit were needed to service the needs of this growing Euro-Canadian population, and many of the land people who were oriented towards an involvement in the "outside" world accepted the employment opportunities that sprang up.

The Tununermiut had traditionally roamed over a vast area of the Canadian eastern Arctic, but they were numerically small. In 1963 there were only fifty-six households among them, and as families moved into the settlement, the camps became more and more sparsely populated. Opportunities for visiting between kinsmen were eroded, and soon others followed the movement to Pond Inlet; thus, in time, an irreversible process was set in motion. The reasons must have been more complex than these few paragraphs suggest, but I believe that what I have listed were the major factors. I turn now to consequences.

Many of the men who had moved into the settlement found employment with the Toonoonik-Sahoonik Co-operative, which for several years had provided municipal services in Pond Inlet. The co-op had contracts with the Settlement Council to provide sewage and garbage pickup and removal, and water and ice delivery to all homes in the settlement. Its sewage and garbage service contract of 1973–74 read in part:

> The Co-operative hereby agrees to provide the Municipal Service of sewage-garbage pickup and removal for all Territorial and Federal Government buildings, Department of National Health and Welfare building, northern rental houses, staff houses, Hudson's Bay Company buildings, and all other buildings as directed by the Pond Inlet Settlement Council and the Settlement Manager or his representative....
> ..."Honey bags" shall be collected daily except Sunday from above buildings and taken to the dump. Garbage shall be collected three times weekly. (Service contract, Toonoonik-Sahoonik Co-operative for 1973-4)

Shortly before I arrived in 1974, there had been a controversy over whether the co-op should continue to provide these services. It was the policy of the Northwest Territories' regional department of local government that all contracts be given to the lowest bidder in an open competition. That year the Settlement Council had itself submitted a bid. Several councillors felt that if they were to operate as a "real" municipal government, *they* should provide the services that were required by the community. However, their bid was higher than that of the co-op, and after a flurry of letters and phone calls between the settlement manager and senior officials in the regional Department of Public Works, the Council was forced to award the contract to the co-op. This decision generated extreme bitterness: councillors openly questioned whether they were a decision-making body or merely the pawn of Euro-Canadian administrators. The incumbent settlement manager strongly supported the council's position and was reprimanded for doing so. Councillors were actively moving towards the acquisition of "hamlet" status for Pond Inlet, which would make it a far more self-governing community at the municipal level, and the rejection of their bid was interpreted as a rejection of this aspiration. However, several of them, including the chair, told me that they planned to try again the following year, and the year after that, until they were successful. At the time I write this, Pond Inlet has been a hamlet for several years.

Traditional sources of employment still existed, such as the HBC. Instead of one Inuit clerk, the Bay now had several full-time Inuit employees. Some of the younger men found work in the school as teaching assistants, and in the lower grades were actually giving instruction in the Inuktitut. They had received training in Yellowknife before taking these positions.

Several men, including Qamaniq, had received training as heavy equipment operators and worked on road building and repair, construction, and so on. In the absence of a resident Euro-Canadian mechanic, Daniellee was in charge of these men and their work activities. Two young men who spoke English fairly well worked as clerks in the government office building, under the direct supervision of the settlement manager, and another, who also worked under the direction of the manager, acted as secretary for the Inuit-managed Housing Association. The Inuit woman who worked in the same building as assistant to the resident social worker was married to a Euro-Canadian school teacher. All four had had several years of formal education in Pond Inlet and residential schools in Churchill, Manitoba, or Frobisher Bay, Northwest Territories. One was the son of a former camp headman, and another the son of a former RCMP special constable. Discussions I had with them indicated that all were ambivalent about office work, but the men, in particular, enjoyed the job security provided by civil service employment.

Some of the older men had casual employment with the De-

Families awaiting departure of children for residential school. Pond Inlet 1973.

Some of the older men had casual employment with the Department of Public Works doing odd jobs around the settlement. I was struck one day to see Arniatsiark, who had been headman in Aullativik ten years earlier, standing on the roof of a house with one of his sons-in-law applying a new coat of tar. He wore coveralls and a baseball cap. Like his oil-rigger son, though, Arniatsiark also hunted when the opportunity presented itself.

With wage employment so prevalent in the settlement, and most children of school age attending the federal day school in Pond Inlet or the residential high school in Frobisher Bay, the Tununermiut were obviously bound by Euro-Canadian conceptions of time in a way that they had not been ten years before. Nevertheless, in the home environment, traditional patterns of time allocation were still practised, leading to a disjointed situation that was at times hard on individuals.

One of the local Euro-Canadian school teachers told me that none of the teachers scheduled important activities for the first half hour of each school day. Students would wake up sleepy-eyed after often only an hour or so of sleep, grab a hunk of bannock, hurriedly drink a cup of tea, and then rush across the settlement to school, usually arriving at least fifteen minutes late. Still — they visiting as well, would then return to bed for an extra hour or two of sleep. The children would often go back to their beds as soon as school finished for the day.

Men usually faced the same problem in the mornings. Qamaniq, who worked under the supervision of Daniellee, once said to me, "I don't always get to work on time. Sometimes I stay up too late at night. I told [Daniellee], 'You can fire me anytime. That's OK.' But he said, 'No, I won't fire you. You are an Eskimo, like me.'" (The older men still used the term "Eskimo.") Daniellee recalled the problems he had experienced years before when, after entertaining camp people in his own home all night, he had had difficulty arriving at work on time the following morning and had regularly been reprimanded by his Euro-Canadian supervisor. Daniellee would often phone Qamaniq and other DPW employees in the morning to awaken them. However, these men also worked regularly on weekends and often returned to work after dinner.

Despite his reliance on wage employment and enjoyment of the material benefits it provided, Qamaniq was not prepared to become subservient and lose his cherished independence. On another occasion he recalled working in Frobisher Bay for a Euro-Canadian foreman who had criticized his work. Qamaniq had replied, "How long have you been in the north? I have been here all my life. This is my country. How long have you been here?"

In summer, when the sun never really sets, Tununermiut sleeping times had always been unregulated. Children would sleep when they felt like it, and their sleeping times did not necessarily coincide with those of their parents. Small children would be supervised by older siblings while parents slept. In general, then, despite the demands of job and school, that pattern was perpetuated in the transformed Pond Inlet. Phones would ring at any time of the night, and people would come and go, visiting friends and relatives until the early hours of the morning. But, except for the sounds of men who had to be "on the job," school children, and Euro-Canadians, a heavy silence lay over the settlement from nine o'clock until almost noon each day.

Traditional patterns of child-training had also been preserved, and the refusal to sternly regulate sleeping hours is, of course, an example of that. Small children continued to live in a totally permissive environment. If a child placed him or herself in a dangerous situation, for example, such as climbing on a tall chair that had been placed on top of a chesterfield and stretching to touch the ceiling, watching parents would stand by ready to avoid a mishap, but would not interfere with the child's activity. Older girls were still responsible for their younger siblings, and it was not uncommon to see girls in early adolescence standing about in *amautiks* (the woman's parka) with infant siblings snuggled into the hoods, and keeping a sharp watch on younger brothers and sisters playing at their feet.

Young girls kept out of the way of brothers, whether a year or so younger, the same age, or older, but they would giggle or smile knowingly when making displays of deference to male egos. Boys, on the other hand, were as demanding of attention as they had been in camps. I saw no evidence of the withering away of male child-training practices that I had witnessed in Aullativik years before, in which boys were abruptly expected to be men, but I wasn't involved in enough settings that included young males to make thorough observations.

Verbal communication in Tununermiut homes was almost exclusively in the Inuktitut, even though most children of school age were fluent in English. The older generations had, in most instances, no more command of English than they had ten years before. A few young married women who had worked for some years for the HBC, or more recently as cooks or housekeepers in the transient centre, were fairly fluent and were more willing than others to use English, but there were not many of these. Even people who ten years before had been oriented towards Euro-Canadian society spoke little English. Most women, in particular, were as unwilling to display any command of English as camp women had been in 1963–64, and it is doubtful whether their fluency was in fact much greater, given the lack of practice.

Although they had accepted formal Euro-Canadian education, many of the older people were still skeptical of whether any values might be derived from it. One elderly woman, who was very prominent in the political structure of the settlement, told me with some vehemence that she was tired of hearing Euro-Canadians say her children needed education. "Of course they have to go to school," she said. "Our children no longer know how to hunt, and when they should be learning to hunt, they are stuck in school. So, because they don't know how to live as Inuits, they *must* keep on going to school. There is no other way today."

Her daughter, who had spent two years in the residential school in Churchill, Manitoba, was typical of many of her generation who had not liked that experience, and in particular had not appreciated being "treated like children." The influence of the "rock generation" had been felt in Pond Inlet, and adolescents preferred to wear their hair long, but in the residential school, they claimed, the hair of both boys and girls had been cut short. They had been placed into groups, I was told, designed as "mixers" to help in adjusting to the school environment, but in fact they had been mixed with children from other settlements rather than with their own friends and relatives, and this only intensified their isolation and loneliness. Anecdotes of this type were quickly elicited from most young people who had spent time in residential high schools. Regardless of the rationale behind these programs, they did contribute to feelings of estrangement from the outside world among youths, and will undoubtedly influence long-range political development in Inuit communities such as Pond Inlet. A high level of religiosity had continued among the Tununermiut almost undiminished through the years. Pond Inlet had developed a reputation in the Canadian Arctic as a particularly religious community. However, the younger people did not show the same degree of fervour as their parents and grandparents, and only a few attended church services regularly. A series of events that occurred in the settlement in 1973 illustrate some consequences of having a reputation as a "religious community."

On August 25, 1973, the HMCS *Protecteur*, flagship of the Canadian fleet, cast anchor in front of the settlement. The purpose of its visit to Pond Inlet and other eastern Arctic settlements was to reinforce the image and reality of Canadian sovereignty in its Arctic waters. In several respects the visit was different from regular yearly visits by government ships such as the *C.D. Howe* insofar as, on its second day, before any of the Euro-Canadian residents had been invited onboard, the members of the Settlement Council were invited for lunch with the captain and his officers. An afternoon party was later held for the entire community, at which hot dogs, cakes, and soft drinks were served by crew members and games held for children. That evening, a party was held in the officer's ward room for Euro-Canadians, so the break with tradition was not complete. I was interested to hear the comments made at the gathering by a helicopter navigator who had attended the dance the community had held the evening before to honour the visitors. (The reason given for the exclusion of Inuit from the evening get-together onboard ship was that alcoholic beverages were to be served, and harmful or embarrassing consequences might result from the behaviour of drunken Inuit. I couldn't help but be reminded of ten years before when a similar rationale was given for excluding Inuit from Euro-Canadian parties.) The navigator had not enjoyed himself at the dance. Two former camp headmen had given presentations of traditional drum dancing, but as neither had used a drum for several decades, the performances evoked more laughter and giggling than respect from the audience. The old men generously joined in the audience response, and after formal greetings had been exchanged between the captain of the *Protecteur* and settlement dignitaries, the dance commenced.

Several members of the crew had fortified themselves generously with alcohol before going ashore, and a few had, illegally, brought bottles to the dance with them. As the evening wore on, visits to the school washroom became more and more frequent, but no one, to my knowledge — crew member or Inuit — became noticeably intoxicated. Since it was Saturday night and dancing was not permitted on Sundays, the dance terminated at midnight instead of continuing through the night, as might otherwise have happened.

The following evening at the party onboard ship, several officers complained that the evening before, the same recording had been played several times in succession. The navigator, whom I referred to earlier, said at one point, "This is supposed to be a very religious community. You can't tell me that, because I saw them last night. Half of them were drunk — didn't you see them at the dance when they got carried away and began to play the same record over and over again? That was when I left!" I replied that there was virtually no liquor in the settlement except in the homes of the Euro-Canadians, as the Inuit who did imbibe had been waiting for days for an aircraft from Resolute Bay with new supplies, but it had not yet arrived, so any alcohol drunk at the dance had been brought ashore by crew members. He denied that this had happened and closed the conversation by stating emphatically, "There is lots of liquor in the settlement, and I know it, because I saw them, and they were drunk. Playing the same record over and over is drunken behaviour." Actually, it is an old tradition dating back to times when Tununermiut owned only a few records. At any rate, so much for the religious reputation the Tununermiut had enjoyed. The navigator and fellow officers spent much of the evening "tossing for drinks."

The impact of the missionaries on the Tununermiut was still dramatic, however, although earlier concerns about secularization following upon modernization had proven somewhat well founded, at least as concerns youth. Several Tununermiut had been ordained as Anglican ministers and had their own parishes. Noah Nashook, resident minister in Igloolik, was one of the first Canadian Inuit to be ordained. The Anglican missionary in Gjoa Haven was a Tununermiut, and Jimmy Muckpah, with whom I had lived ten years before, was minister in Eskimo Point. All had their theological training in Pangnirtung. Conversations I had with the missionary in Pond Inlet in 1973 indicated that the Pond Inlet people who had received this training had been extremely influential with their fellow trainees. He identified Jimmy Muckpah in particular. Despite Jimmy's hunting skills, I had not known him as a man who dominated others, and so I attributed his influence to the intense religious attitudes he had demonstrated years before. In the summer of 1973, two other Tununermiut, Benjamin Arreak and Jonas Allooloo, were studying for the ministry in Pangnirtung. In Resolute Bay, which was by then a mixed Inuit community of people from Pond Inlet and Spence Bay, the lay preacher was a former Aullativikmiut, Kadloo, who had already left for Resolute before I arrived in 1963.

Two men had emerged as leaders of Pond Inlet's Anglican mission: Timothy Kadlu and Koonook Pitseeolok. Kadloo had been headman at the Bylot Island camp, Illukisaat, ten years earlier, and I had mistakenly identified him as a potential leader of a revitalization movement because of his rejection of Euro-Canadian lifestyles. He was still highly respected by his fellow Tununermiut, and he still did not live a life of conspicuous consumption, but he had joined the exodus from the land to the settlement and, aside from a brief period of activity in local settlement politics, had settled down in his old age to a life of religious involvement. There was, then, a certain continuity between his earlier period as a lay preacher in his camp and his present position. The changes had, I believe, understandably been too fast for him, and he had adapted by holding on to beliefs integral to him.

Pitseeolok, the eldest son of a headman, had been a close friend of Jimmy Muckpah and a first cousin of his wife, Elisapee; he worked as a clerk in the HBC store but was also catechist for the mission. A tall, handsome man of husky build, he regularly gave the weekly sermon at services in the Anglican mission but he was not active in other settlement organizations. I find it easy to speculate that the Anglicans who were actively involved with the mission's activities represented one form of Tununermiut efforts to preserve elements of the contact-traditional period in a time of rapid change, whether they did so consciously or not, but possibly I am too prone to look for vestiges of that earlier time.

On the other hand, young leaders were emerging in the mission who were not from camp backgrounds. One of these, a young man who was a special constable with the RCMP and whose father had been a special constable for a decade or more, may be representative of an effort on the part of Euro-Canadian–oriented Tununermiut to regain the community status lost when camp people dominated the local political structure. The mission had become, in certain respects, then, a locus for involvement of Tununermiut of several stripes, because of the role it had played in the acculturative process they had experienced over time, and the possibilities it provided for a balance between the two worlds that the more religious males found themselves torn between.

Women were very active in mission activities; according to the resident Anglican missionary, more so than men. In some cases, the women had husbands who had low status in the community, but there were other reasons as well for female involvement. Ten years before, camp women had, when men were absent, displayed considerable motivation to interact with one another. They enjoyed one another's company and took pleasure in being together – one woman making a new parka for a child, another making bannock for her family, and others simply sitting close and participating in the talk. Once established within the settlement, they seemed to find that the mission offered an arena for continuing these interactions, and a focus for their energies. This was an arena from which they were not excluded, one that encouraged their involvement and regular attendance. However, they were also not systematically excluded from the political arena, and many were more than willing to strive for political position.

The overall impression one received of Pond Inlet in 1973, as I have suggested earlier, was similar to what one would have gained from a visit to small prairie towns and villages in the Canadian west or rural Ontario or fishing villages in the Maritimes. The Hudson's Bay Company store was like a typical general store, selling everything from yard goods to fishing equipment to candy, and was visited each day by virtually every woman in the settlement, who came to hear the latest gossip as well as to browse through the displays. The Anglican mission was the social centre of the community in many respects, and most people still retained at least a vestigial tie with the fundamentalist theology it supported. There were a few dogteams chained to stakes at one end of the settlement, but most men owned snowmobiles. (Several dogs were kept as "pets" but spent most of their lives tied to short ropes outside the homes of their owners. They were the offspring of dogs that had been brought north to the settlement by Euro-Canadians.) Children moved freely back and forth between houses, eating lunch at home one day, at the home of an aunt the next, and at the home of a school friend on the third. Men who had employment in the settlement would walk home for tea at morning and afternoon break-times, bringing with them fellow workers, and they would sit around kitchen tables smoking and drinking tea until it was time to return to work.

A major innovation in the settlement was the community-owned and -operated radio station. This station had had a chequered history, and its right to exist has been debated in the Canadian Parliament and discussed in *Time* magazine. In the mid-1960s a Dutch equipment mechanic with the DNANR who was a short-wave radio hobbyist began to use his own transmitter to play recordings, which were picked up by local radios. In a sense, he was operating a "pirate" radio station on the "ham" band. When he left the settlement, as Euro-Canadians usually do in time, he sold his equipment to some Tununermiut, who continued the practice of broadcasting recordings and also began to intersperse them with messages and conversation. Repeated attempts to close down the "station" were unsuccessful, and in time the question whether it should be legalized or not was debated in Parliament. Here was a case of grass-roots, almost indigenous development of a technical operation that was increasingly of benefit to the community in which it was located. The CBC station in Frobisher Bay gave strong written and moral support to the operators of the Pond Inlet station, and eventually it was given a license.

A young Tununermiut man who had grown up in the settlement was appointed station manager in the spring of 1968 and sent to Frobisher Bay for training in station management. It was not long before disagreements between the young manager and the directors of the station led to his dismissal, but by that time the station's future was secure. It had become a permanent part of settlement life.

In 1973 there were several part-time announcers who worked the microphone and turntable each noon and evening. One was Arnaviapik, a former headman, who showed an amazing talent for adaptation. Arnaviapik was aged, but he had regular employment as a disk jockey with the local radio station, and his voice could be heard daily in every Inuit home in the settlement, introducing records and passing on gossip and other information.

The music played at the station tended to be heavily weighted towards country and western, but in general depended on the whims and tastes of the individual announcer. News of approaching aircraft was announced, as were community events and other activities and happenings. News was broadcast about people who were out of the settlement and had written to friends or relatives, and notification was given to individuals who had received but not collected mail. (One of the announcers, a younger brother of Qamaniq, was married to the local postmistress, and the post office was attached to their home.) All broadcasting was done in Inuktitut, which probably disturbed Euro-Canadians, who regularly heard recordings interrupted by announcements in a language most could not understand. Radios were still important and central items in Tununermiut homes, and the local Pond Inlet station was a consolidating force in the community. When in operation, it could be heard in almost every Inuit home in the settlement.

The ancient pattern of reciprocity, which has long been a dominant theme in Inuit culture and social relationships, was vitally retained in the transformed Pond Inlet. This was particularly noticeable during the latter part of the summer of 1973, while the community residents awaited the arrival of supply ships and the celebrative time of sealift. As I mentioned earlier, because the HBC store was depleted of all foodstuffs other than a few nonessential items, the people were once again dependent on "land" food. When men had time in the evenings or on weekends, they would go out in their canoes to hunt seal or travel inland in search of caribou. In particular, workers for Pan-Arctic would make use of their rest-and-recuperation periods to hunt and fish. Many of the men, however, no longer owned canoes. (When Qamaniq and I discussed the idea of a return trip to Aullativik, he said that he would have to rent a canoe if we decided to go. In the end, it was not possible to rent one, as all were being used for hunting.) Men who did have meat, however, were quick to share it with others.

I recall several times when women or men would turn up at Qamaniq's door with a hunk of seal or caribou meat, which they would set on the floor and then leave. Similarly, on the two occasions when Qamaniq returned from evening hunts with fresh seal meat — he travelled with Daniellee in the latter's canoe — he distributed sections to his kinsmen. The regularity with which children ate at the homes of relatives and friends is another measure of reciprocity. (Elsewhere I have described the manner in which alcohol has become a mechanism for the perpetuation of traditional relations based on reciprocity [Matthiasson 1974]). During the short second time I had in Pond Inlet it was impossible to trace the networks of individuals and groups involved in these patterns of reciprocity; my point is simply that we have here one more example of the perpetuation of cultural forms in a town setting — forms that pre-date the contact-traditional period in Tununermiut history. These patterns were in fact resources that could be drawn upon in times of crisis, such as a food shortage, and allowed for continuity in a context of drastic change.

The Political Scene

In 1963 Pond Inlet's area administrator considered that it was still too early to form a Settlement or Community Council, and instead put his energies into developing a local co-operative. By 1973 both had been formed and had undergone several phases of growth and change. My main reasons for returning to the settlement was to examine political change and the emergence or, possibly more properly, the evolution of Tununermiut-based political leadership. I was particularly interested in whether these political developments, if in fact they had occurred, had been outgrowths of, or maintained continuity with, the political systems that had operated in the camps ten years before. I was also interested in the role that the Euro-Canadian–oriented Tununermiut of ten years before had played in any political reshapings.

The four organizations in Pond Inlet that were overtly political were the Community Council, composed of six persons; the Toonoonik-Sahoonik Cooperative, with a seven-person board of directors; the Hunters and Trappers Association, which had a six-person executive board; and the Housing Association, comprising six executive members and a clerk. The Community Council was the most openly political. Under the close supervision of area administrators (who were later replaced by settlement managers) and, more recently, the adult education director, the Council had nevertheless displayed over its short life a capacity for decision-making that belies the popular notion of such societies as having totally diffuse and non-hierarchical political systems. (The adult education director in 1973, a Euro-Canadian as had been all of his predecessors, was an elected member of the Council.)

The Council was formed in 1965, the Co-operative in 1969, the Housing Association in 1970, and the Hunters and Trappers Association the following year. The first chair of the first three organizations was Maktar, a man of immense traditional prestige, who had worked for several years for the DNANR. He was chair of the Community Council for three years and then vice-chair for four years. The men who replaced him in these positions were close personal friends of his who would regularly seek his advice on major decisions. Maktar, although a Roman Catholic in an Anglican community, bridged the two worlds of the land-oriented peoples of the last decade and those who found satisfaction in allegiances with Euro-Canadians, perhaps more effectively than any other Tununermiut. The first chair of the Hunters and Trappers Association was John Tongak, the son of Timothy Kadlu, who had been a headman a decade before and who I had thought might lead a revitalization movement.

For a brief period those Tununermiut oriented towards Euro-Canadian styles had become dominant in political organizations, but their influence was temporary and they were soon replaced by camp people who had attained prestige and status through conventional means as hunters, providers, and decision-makers. Former camp headmen took a brief turn as participants in these organizations, but, probably because of their age, they were replaced by younger men. Strangely enough, to me at least, Qamaniq was not involved in the leadership of any of these organizations, although his name was often put forward as a nominee for one or another. I attribute this to his long-standing rivalry with Maktar. Maktar's earlier movement into the settlement seems to have put him in a position of advantage over Qamaniq. His leadership in one organization coupled with the support of resident Euro-Canadians carried over into his bids for prominent positions in the Co-operative and Housing Association. However, it was his status as a "traditional" Inuit that made possible his retention of these positions.

Daniellee, the long-term DNANR employee, had always maintained his relationship with the people living in camps, and this made it possible for him to move from vice-chair of the Co-operative in its third year to Chair for 1972 and 1973. Like Maktar, he had spanned the distance between the two worlds of the Tununermiut. His aloof handling of contacts with Euro-Canadians had "paid off"; by maintaining his posture as his own man, he had retained his status in the traditional Tununermiut hierarchy. It must be remembered that positions in these organizations are elected. Euro-Canadians retain ultimate rights to manipulate the decisions made by these bodies, but the more insightful ones recognized that the political acumen displayed by Inuit members was an indication of future trends, and gave their support to the decisions that came out of meetings. Certainly, the incumbent settlement manager in 1973 did his best to respect council decisions.

Women's place in the political scene had been little influenced by any of the developments of the contact-traditional period. Once the population had moved into the settlement and new political organizations were formed, however, women began to put forth their conception of their place in the political realm. That place was not inconsequential. Sula Kubla, the mother of Maktar and

Paul Koolerk (then the elected member of the Territorial Council for the high Arctic), was the most prominent. I remember a chance encounter with her one evening: she remembered me but wasn't sure where we had met before. Paul, who had become a close friend of myself and my family during the several years he had lived in Ottawa, was away at Yellowknife for a set of committee meetings and so was not available to help us rekindle our friendship. She invited me in for a cup of tea and we sat and enjoyed one another's company as she told me about the effects of rapid change among the Tununermiut, most of which annoyed and disturbed her. She had been on the board of directors of the co-operative for the past three years.

An older sister of Qamaniq had also been interested in electoral office but was not immediately successful. Her name appeared on several ballot forms for the Council and the Co-operative. In 1971 she was elected to the board of directors of the Co-operative and continued in that capacity for the next two years. Over time, she and Sula Kubla were joined by several other women.

The Housing Association was in many respects as important in the life of Pond Inlet as the Council. It definitely had more autonomy. Houses in the settlement were available to residents on a rental basis, and it was the members of the Housing Association who determined who would live where and what their rental fees would be. In general, those members employed fair and equitable methods of reaching their decisions: the possessor of a well-paid job might pay twice as much each month as a widow with a large family, even though her house was twice the size of his. In 1973, three of the six members of the Housing Association were women.

The Hunters and Trappers Association had only been operative for three years in 1973, but it was rapidly gaining prominence in the settlement's political affairs. Its executive was composed largely of young men, and it was under the close tutelage of Elijah Erkloo, its secretary-treasurer, who had spent several years in Ottawa acting as an interpreter for the DNANR and as assistant on a project for the development of a new Roman orthography for the Inuit language. He later resided for a few years in Frobisher Bay. One of the first Tununermiut to leave the Arctic, on his return to Pond Inlet Elijah had been instrumental in establishing interest in a "return to nature." He enjoyed taking groups of young boys out during summer months on hunting and fishing expeditions and teaching them land lore. Working with the Adult Education Program as an assistant director gave him opportunities to indulge himself in these activities, and enabled him to work closely with the Hunters and

Trappers Association. One of the particular interests of members of the Association was the question of aboriginal land rights, which was to become the major Inuit political topic in the following decades.

In the time that elapsed between 1963 and 1973, the Tununermiut did not experience the revitalization movement I had predicted. Events during that time had been too fast moving and cataclysmic to allow for such a development. However, things were beginning to stabilize, and with this stabilization was emerging a new interest in the past. The activities of individuals such as Elijah Erkloo and organizations such as the Hunters and Trappers Association were not the only examples of that interest: men hunted on weekends and evenings not only because their families needed the meat, but also because they took pride in hunting and found personal satisfaction in it. Daniellee, who was entitled to a yearly paid vacation in Montreal for himself and his family, told me that he planned, in the summer of 1973, to take his family out on the land on a combined camping and hunting trip. He wanted the peace and tranquility of a sojourn on the land, rather than the fast pace of Montreal. His sentiments were not atypical (although the fact that his wife had died a few years earlier, a victim of a too-rapid pace of acculturation, probably played no small part in his continued attachment to traditional values).

The contact-traditional period had passed, and after one more times of forced change brought about by contact with the outside world, the Tununermiut were regrouping their resources. Their men worked on oil rigs but hunted in their spare time. These men moved easily between commuting hundreds of miles back and forth from their work sites, to solitary walks over vast stretches of ice in search of the seal, the animal that their fathers and grandfathers had hunted. Men such as Elijah Erkloo and Paul Koolerk, who had experienced the outside world and rejected it, returned to Pond Inlet and became new-style leaders, working closely with men who had only moved from camps to settlement but had brought with them the political skills they had acquired in a more traditional setting.

Paul was the first Inuk to be elected to the Council of the Northwest Territories from the high Arctic. He was not the last. He succeeded primarily through Inuit support. Pond Inlet has since become a hamlet, and its community Council a municipal government, able to act in a more autonomous fashion. Its members have drawn on traditional forms of political behaviour in their deliberations, but also have at their disposal the skills they have inherited from the contact situation. Their young people know who they are. They are Tununermiut, and although they are irrevocably a part of the modern world, they are still the sons of hunters. Even the centralization period has now been transcended.

When I left Pond Inlet in 1963 I travelled to Resolute Bay onboard the *C.D. Howe*. The few Inuit onboard with me were going for tuberculosis treatment in southern hospitals. They travelled in the lower decks of the ship, in isolation, and were filled with fear (although they disguised it) at the seemingly interminable time separation they faced from their families and friends. When I left in 1973 I travelled by aircraft to Resolute Bay. With me on the flight were several young Tununermiut who were journeying on a holiday to Arctic Bay where they would visit relatives. As I watched them step from the plane, I thought back to the earlier time. The old men who had been camp headmen preferred the past. These young men and women seemed in control of the present. The future was another story, and it is being realized today. The Tununermiut, like Inuit across the Canadian arctic, seem to be once again in control of their own destiny, and I wish them well.

EPILOGUE

Changes in Identity and Politics

I have tried to describe a period of rapid and profound change undergone by the Tununermiut, during which they experienced a mass uprooting and migration to the settlement, and its attendant transformation of their personal lives. The context within which these changes occurred was not created by the Tununermiut themselves — it was imposed from without. The people had to respond to it and, as they moved into the settlement, to learn to cope with institutions with which they had previously been only somewhat familiar. Some observers may claim that the move was a conscious one, and that they chose the new ways of life. In part, of course, that is true. Perhaps they could have resisted the pull to the settlement. What is more important, in my opinion, is that they handled the move in their own ways, rather than being passively manipulated by outside forces.

In the text I have for the most part shied away from discussion of anthropological issues of theory and methodology, but a brief examination of one of those issues is appropriate here. The issue concerns acculturation studies — ones that focus on societies affected by external intervention from militarily more powerful societies — which were popular in anthropology during the time the Tununermiut and other Canadian Inuit were moving into settlements. Most anthropologists today recognize that cultural systems are dynamic and in constant flux, and that humans, rather than being blown about by the winds of change, are creative and can exercise some freedom in their responses. That is, they can be both flexible and creative. Social and cultural change from this perspective are indeed creative processes. I submit that the Tununermiut used their own freedom in determining how they would manage town living. Today such a statement is almost trite, but it does not fit the tenets of most of the early writers on acculturation.

Still, freedom and creativity in this sense are not without limits. In many situations of the fairly recent past, the heavy hand of colonial administration has forced change in directions that have been sharply circumscribed. The abrupt changes experienced by the Tununermiut, as well as all other Inuit populations across Arctic Canada during the second half of this century, seemed harbingers of a new and more constricting colonial yoke.

During the contact-traditional period, there had certainly been a colonial quality to the Tununermiut's relation with the RCMP, missionaries, and traders. At the same time, the Tununermiut continued to live on the land and so maintained considerable control over their own lives. They were in fact economically dependent upon the traders – in this instance, the HBC – and they had accepted Christianity and paid at least titular homage to the authority of the police. But out on the land, in the camps or while on hunting trips, they were under the surveillance of no one except other Inuit.

At the time of the relocation, most observers took a pessimistic view, predicting that Inuit society would fall apart as the people settled into settlement life. Demoralization and the erosion of individual self-esteem were sure to be the consequences. Acculturation theory of that period supported such a prediction, and published studies provided many empirical examples. It was generally accepted that no human society could for long withstand the onslaught of an alien and colonially oriented force. Aboriginal societies were thought to be no match for colonial systems, and seemed doomed to either assimilate into the larger society or disintegrate. Either eventuality would lead to the subordinate society's loss of its traditional basis for self-determination and its cultural collapse. Cultures were generally regarded, then, as fragile entities; tradition on its own was not enough to sustain cultural identity and viability.

I do not think that I state the case too strongly. Much of the anthropology of the Canadian Arctic that was written in the 1960s and 1970s reflected this pessimistic and doom-saying perspective. The ethnographic accounts were valid, but when their authors looked to the future the prospect for Inuit culture was grim – it was only a matter of time before it disappeared.

One notable exception to this theoretical stance, and one that dealt with the North American Arctic, was an article by Norman Chance (Chance, 1960). I can recall, as a graduate student at Cornell University, an encounter with Lauriston Sharp, who as much as anyone had created the pessimistic stance with his publications on cultural breakdown among aboriginal Australians. He told me in an excited way one day that Chance had published a case in which an aboriginal population had been able to cope effectively with rapid acculturation. Other works on Arctic North Americans of the time tended to ignore Chance's work. Perhaps the data of the ethnographers forced them to make dire predictions, but I am convinced that it was more the intellectual climate of anthropology of the time, and the widely accepted acculturation paradigm.

For a while, I shared the negative perspective myself, although even in the late 1960s I felt uncomfortable with the position. My own thoughts about the future of the Inuit were predicated on my experiences living in a camp under the tutelage of men and women of whom I stood in real awe. They were not likely, in my opinion, to sink under the new regime imposed by Ottawa and Yellowknife even if they did leave the land. I expected that there would be casualties with the adjustments to settlement life, but I was also convinced that the people would persevere and, in the end, survive.

On at least one occasion, my optimism led me astray: I published an article in which I argued that the Tununermiut had learned to use alcoholic beverages in a way that did not necessarily involve regular abuse (Matthiasson, 1974). I claimed that they had come to treat alcohol as a scarce resource used much as meat had been in more traditional times. In the year in which this article was published, there were four alcohol-related deaths in Pond Inlet. I still believe in my original thesis, but I had obviously missed the darker side of the Tununermiut's introduction to alcohol.

Granted the tragically high human costs to them of access to alcohol and other drugs, the Tununermiut have demonstrated their characteristic ingenuity by creating novel ways to decrease that price. At the time of writing, there exist in Pond Inlet both a Community Alcohol Education Program and an Alcohol Education Committee, both of which regulate the availability of alcohol to community residents. They were established after the holding of two liquor plebiscites, in 1975 and 1977, when citizens had become increasingly concerned about alcohol and drug abuse. As a result, anyone who wishes to bring alcohol into the community must first appear before the committee and convince members that he or she does not have an alcohol problem. Those with identified problems, and those who are known to supply liquor to such persons, are interdicted and thus denied the right to consume alcohol legally.

In a small, isolated community such as Pond Inlet it is relatively simple to enforce such regulations, for liquor must be brought in by air, and the RCMP can meet all incoming aircraft and inspect baggage. Whether or not the regulations assist in controlling the making of home brew is, I am afraid, another question, and it is less easy to keep out soft drugs such as marijuana. Nevertheless, the general optimism I had felt about Tununermiut responses to the introduction of alcohol may not have been completely without foundation, although it took the creation of an innovative program to work through the problems. Abuse of alcohol and other drugs as a way of coping with rapid change in acculturative situations is not uncommon. I have been told that other Inuit communities are considering adopting the Pond Inlet model of alcohol control.

In his widely read ethnography on social and economic change among the Inuit of Sugluk, Nelson Graburn (1969) epitomized the negative predictions about Inuit life in the settlements. While he obviously was saddened by the destruction of a way of life, he seemed to be saying that the colonial forces were so structured and powerful that the Inuit would have little opportunity to regain political control of their own lives. On the contrary, I submit, the formation of a committee to deal with internal problems of alcohol and drug use reflects a sense of political self-determination among the people of Pond Inlet. Other responses of the Tununermiut that I have chronicled here also raise questions about Graburn's conclusions, although of course, the pan-Inuit movement did not emerge until well after the book was published.

The Emergence of a New Political Paradigm

The names by which we refer to ourselves or others can also be used to manipulate our identity and to align with or isolate ourselves from others, as well as to rationalize our treatment of others. When I lived with the Aullativikmiut in the 1960s they referred to themselves as Eskimos, as did all of the Tununermiut. By the 1970s many of them had ceased to use the term, which was now considered pejorative. (Its etymological origins have always been murky, although many sources claim that it means "eaters of raw meat.") It was, of course, replaced in both singular and plural by Inuk and Inuit, for "a person," and "the people." The change in terminology of self-reference had, I am convinced, enormous political significance.

Not everyone accepted the change readily, and in some instances it was never adopted. One elderly man who had lived virtually all of his life in the camps told me in 1973, "I was born an Eskimo and I will die an Eskimo." However, his was to become a minority position. Others — even of his generation — soon saw the political significance of rejecting the term, and certainly that man's children and grandchildren did.

This change, which was so important in the construction of new individual and group identities, was the work of The Inuit Tapirisat of Canada (ITC), or Inuit Brotherhood, a new organization that sought to create a pan-Inuit consciousness. The ITC was external to the Tununermiut, but when it offered them a new political agenda they responded, and in the process took further steps towards a renewed sense of self-determination.

Formed in Ottawa in 1971 after a meeting that gathered together Inuit from across Canada and from many walks of life, the *ITC* began as an educational organization but over time became increasingly political in its overall policy and specific objectives. Not long after its formation it became perhaps the most potent political force in the Northwest Territories.

Until the formation of the ITC, Tununermiut contacts with the world outside their own territory — ones that, as we have seen, led to many internal adjustments — had been with non-Inuit. Now they would encounter a new force from the outside. It was one with roots in the Arctic, and the personnel who carried it forward were themselves Inuit. These new encroachers preached a political ideology — one that sought unification of all Canadian Inuit within a common purpose and consciousness. The traditional boundaries of the larger -*miut* groups were to be broken down and replaced by a sense of shared identity. One of their primary goals, which was put forward not long after the formation of the ITC, was the establishment of a new, ethnically-based territory within the Canadian high Arctic, which would be largely an Inuit domain.

Nunavut, that new Jerusalem of the Arctic, may well become a reality, and if it does it will encompass approximately one-fifth of the land mass of Canada. The concept has been shepherded by the Tungavik Federation of Nunavut, an auxiliary of the ITC. Using geographers, anthropologists, and lawyers, the Federation has developed a strong case, and at the time of writing has been ratified in principal by the federal government and the Council of the Northwest Territories. A plebiscite on partition was held in 1992 in the Northwest Territories; the vote was strongly in favour of partition in Nunavut itself, but overall there was only a slim majority in favour of it. In the Mackenzie district, some opposition to partition was based on economic concerns related to the loss of resources in Nunavut, while other opposition emanated from the Dene nation, which perceived that the proposed boundary in the western Arctic islands infringed on their land claims and sovereignty.

The ITC has not maintained its hold on all Inuit. As happens in many organizations, splintering has been common among Canadian aboriginal political associations. In 1973 the Inuvialuit of the western regions broke off from ITC and began negotiating land claims on their own. They reached a major agreement with the federal government in 1984, but its conditions are much less broad than those envisioned in the concept of Nunavut.

In spite of political factionalism, the ITC's influence on most Canadian Inuit, including the Tununermiut, has been considerable. It has done much more than provide them with a new name, although that was extremely important symbolically. It also gave them a nation-wide power base in their own efforts towards local forms of self-determination. The ITC, then, has been a major factor in the Tununermiut's ability to withstand the negative effects of colonialism.

I believe that after their relocation to Pond Inlet the Tununermiut employed a traditional response to their changed circumstances; that is, initially they adopted a "wait and see" posture, which involved studying the new parameters of their lives and thoughtfully examining different long-range options. It may have been this stance that misled some observers into making pessimistic predictions about their future. They did not at first seem to be taking control of matters. This tendency to stand back and evaluate alternatives before acting is, in my opinion, a trait firmly rooted in Inuit child-training practices and expressed in adult personality. (McConnell [1976] has described this pattern in somewhat different terms.)

With the advent of the ITC, a course of action was presented and, for the most part, accepted by the Tununermiut. The ITC role, a crucial one, was to politically mobilize the Tununermiut. However — and this is more a statement of faith than of fact — I suggest that the Tununermiut would in time have created their own revitalization movement with or without the ITC. The beginnings of such a movement were apparent in the early 1970s. Perhaps what was taking place was similar to events among Indians to the south, who are turning to their elders for knowledge of tradition. The Tununermiut may not have continued to elect former camp bosses to formal leadership roles, but they recognized their importance as links with the past.

At the same time as they began efforts to retain parts of traditional culture in the settlement context, individuals began to take advantage of new economic opportunities. There is evidence of this in the several young Tununermiut who became entrepreneurs. Qamaniq and his taxi service is a notable example.

I am suggesting that even without the ITC, although it certainly was an asset, the Tununermiut might have adopted the posture of ethnicity on their own. This is not only a posture, but also a strategy — one in which a population that is a small part of a much larger political and economic system strives to maintain features of its traditional identity, while at the same time taking advantage of the perceived benefits the larger system offers. The position involves selectivity; some features of the old and the new are selected for retention and use and forged into a new synthesis, and some elements of both are rejected. It involves a population's assuming responsibility for the contours of their own cultural existence.

Nevertheless, the ITC has been of enormous assistance to the Tununermiut as they have created their own ethnic identity within Canada. If nothing else, it plugged this relatively isolated community into a network of similar communities with like aspirations stretching across Arctic Canada.

A Larger Matrix – Inuit Among Other Aboriginals

The aboriginal peoples of Canada — both Inuit and Indian — have long been hidden from view, and when presented to the larger population, they often appear in stereotypical terms. The Inuit, for example, have been described in many elementary and secondary school textbooks as a quaint and romantic people who live in snow houses and eat raw meat. Until recently, few Canadians from the south visited the high Arctic, and that was possibly advantageous to the Inuit. Even after huge amounts of federal resources were pumped into the Arctic during the times described herein, the average Canadian knew little or nothing about those expenditures, their effects, or the people who experienced those effects. I have found that Canadian university students often do not know the difference between the Yukon and Northwest Territories, or where to place Baffin Island on a map of Canada.

Indians, on the other hand, live in regions of the country that have seen dense settlement by outsiders, yet have typically been cloistered away on isolated reserves or ghetto-ized in the cities. The varied Indian populations have long been the target of discriminatory attitudes held by Canadians who, in most cases, have never knowingly met a person of Indian ancestry.

The realities of life for both aboriginal peoples have long been hidden from societal view, then, and few Canadians have seemed to care much about that. All this began to change in the 1980s, and it was a most dramatic time for Indians.

A major shift in the Canadian collective consciousness was part of these events, and, in my opinion constituted a major catalyst — that is, Canadians began to think of their nation as multicultural. Waves of immigrants from non-European parts of the world had begun to flood into Canada and had become vocal about their right to retain their cultural identities. The federal government and professional social observers realized as well that the original immigrants, most of whom had come from Europe, had not "melted together." Instead, they had carved out ethnic niches for themselves in what was coming to be called the Canadian mosaic. That which "was" was transformed into that which "should be," and soon ethnic diversity became not only a sociological fact but something encouraged by governing bodies at federal and provincial levels. New funding sources for ethnic groups were established, along with agencies to administer them.

I suggest that aboriginal peoples looked at these new policies and the multicultural ideology behind them and asked about their own place in the mosaic. Their conclusion was easily reached — they had been left out once again. Their exclusion may reflect an underlying assumption long held by the federal government, and its agencies geared to deal with aboriginal "problems," that in time both Indian and Inuk would be absorbed into the larger society. Their policies seemed to be directed towards this end. Obviously assimilation has not yet happened.

In response to this new ideology, aboriginal organizations were established at all levels, from the local to the national. Matters were, of course, more complex than I have indicated here, but the idea of ethnic self-determination was without doubt one important factor spurring aboriginal peoples to form and justify their own indigenous associations. Such organizations proliferated during the 1970s and 1980s, with the ITC being one of them. However, their activities did not capture the public imagination, other than sporadically, until 1990, when two events catapulted aboriginal peoples onto centre stage.

The first event was the blocking of the Meech Lake Accord, a proposal to create a new relationship between the federal and provincial governments. The details are not relevant here, but in the popular mind the Accord's failure was due to the actions of Elijah Harper, the only aboriginal member of the Manitoba legislature. Day after day the media reported on Harper's refusal to vote in favour of ratification. His stated reason for opposition was that the bill did not take into account aboriginal concerns, and aboriginal leaders had not been included in deliberations between the federal government and the provinces. He became a national hero and a symbolic leader of the movement for greater recognition of aboriginal rights in Canada.

The second event was the confrontation at Oka, Quebec. A dispute had arisen between residents of the Kahnawake Mohawk reserve and a municipality adjacent to it, over a proposed golf course. The Mohawks claimed that the land on which the course was to be constructed was a traditional burial ground. When a resolution could not be reached, the Mohawk Warrior Society formed a blockade of overturned automobiles and created a stand-off. Again, I must gloss over the details of a complex and many-layered situation, but the confrontation went on for some time and received nightly attention from the national television networks.

Suddenly, aboriginal peoples in Canada were no longer hidden away; because of these two events, they were the main subject of the news. Native leaders were in both instances interviewed regularly, and for the first time the average Canadian could see them as highly articulate and intelligent men and women, whether they were the supporters of Elijah Harper, dressed in business suits, or the Warriors and their women supporters at Oka, clad in guerilla garb and wearing masks. These were wholly contrasting images, but both won nation-wide sympathy. Their arguments, presented through the media, were found to be compelling and, for many listeners, convincing. The person viewing late-night news may not have fully understood the intricacies of the issues, and may have sympathized with the Indians because of his or her own frustrations with federal policies and the place of Quebec in Canada. Be that as it may, my point is that there was an outpouring of support. Those same leaders, having at least temporarily captured the interest of the media, publicly vowed that never again would their people and their concerns be hidden from public consciousness.

I do not know what effects the events of 1990 had on the Tununermiut and other Inuit. However, they have television sets in their homes and receive signals from satellite at the same instant as viewers in Halifax and Vancouver. Their youth understand the language of the nightly news broadcasts and translate it for their elders. If those events had a powerful effect on the consciousness of Indians across Canada, it is likely that they have also influenced the thinking of the Inuit — thinking, that is, about their own place in contemporary Canada, and about land rights, open dialogue, and even nationhood. Certainly the Indians are now referring to themselves as sovereign nations. Whether Nunavut will, in the long run, be seen by the Inuit of the eastern Arctic as something more than a new territory to be governed like the provinces and the other territories, may be more than merely a rhetorical question.

My reason for venturing into the larger discourse of native consciousness and aspirations is to try to illustrate the place of aboriginal peoples — both Indian and Inuit — in the Canadian nation-state as the twenty-first century approaches. That place has been challenged, legally and politically, by the people themselves. The Inuit responses have been more cautious, perhaps, but that may be only one more example of the "wait and see" approach to unfolding events. The rest of the country itself must now wait and see.

The Present

While the position of aboriginal peoples in the larger society evolved and shifted at many levels, Pond Inlet and its Tununermiut residents, although undoubtedly influenced by those events, continued to cope with more evolutionary, as opposed to revolutionary, changes. These have in many respects been more incremental. For instance, the settlement itself continues to be gradually transformed. The adjustments made by Inuit residents have in part been shaped by efforts to hold on to traditional ways — the ways of their nomadic ancestors — but they have also been creative, involving innovative adaptations. Given their circumstances, the people have once again demonstrated their ingenuity.

As I mentioned earlier, when I first arrived in the tiny settlement in 1963 there was not even a landing strip for incoming aircraft. We landed on the muskeg behind a hill, and no one knew of our landing other than a few birds who flew away in panic at the approach of our small craft. Today the permanent runway is part of a full-scale airport, with its own weather station, that receives several aircraft every week. How the Tununermiut use this new facility to achieve their own ends is for others to document.

In 1963 there was a small, one-room nursing station but no nurse; the resident RCMP officer provided medical services. That building has long since been replaced by a large nursing station, with a permanent nursing staff. Along with Inuit in other communities, the Tununermiut are seeking ways to maximize the benefits of health services. Efforts to decentralize medical resources, to base them within the community, are an indication of this move, as well as an example of the drive for greater self-determination.

Instead of all recreational activities taking place in the gymnasium of the school, there is a community hall and a covered arena for sporting events. The local schools have enrolments of several hundred students, the teaching staffs include well-qualified Inuit, and the curricula have Inuktitut-language instruction and Inuit-culture modules.

By 1989 the population of Pond Inlet was almost nine hundred, and growing, a far cry indeed from the early 1960s when the Inuit lived on the land and the settlement population numbered only a couple of dozen people. Local councils and communities have been creative in finding ways to cope with this demographic explosion.

In 1963 I spent my first night in Pond Inlet in a teacherage, empty during the summer vacation. Ten years later I stayed in a newly constructed transient centre, and the other temporary boarders and I slept in bunks side by side and made our own make-shift meals with supplies purchased at the Bay store. Now there is a hotel with its own dining room. This facility is part of a new thrust in the community. Its economic base, although mixed, is primarily tourism, and the local Co-operative maintains a fishing lodge at Koluktoo Bay as well as providing package tours of the area and special tours of the bird sanctuary on Bylot Island. The latter has become a pilgrimage site for amateur bird-watchers and professional ornithologists from around the world. Seeing all of this, I remember when Kayak was laughed at for spending his savings from years of service with the RCMP on a large boat that he planned to use to transport visiting government officials and scientists about the area.

Hunting continues to be one source of food for the Tununermiut; far more so than was the case in 1973, when it seemed to have almost died out. Today men take their children out with them to hunt on weekends and during vacations. Entire families go back to the land for short periods to re-enact the camp life of the past, and so youngsters do not have to learn outdoor living skills from teachers imported from the south, as I saw happening in 1973.

The people have not forgotten that their forefathers were hunters and that their identities — both male and female — were forged within a hunting existence. I have been told that some Tununermiut are even returning to the use of dogs and sleds for their hunting expeditions, in place of snowmobiles. Aside from their practical value, the former are symbols of a sense of continuity with the past. Hunters may use better rifles or sleep in tents bought by mail order instead of hand-sewn from canvas, but the Tununermiut have always been quick to pick up on more efficient artifacts and technologies, and that has nothing to do with knowing who they are.

Change has continued to pursue the Tununermiut, then, but in so many ways they seem to be in control of it. It would be wrong of me to try and present here all the changes that are still in process, for I have not done field work among them for too long a time. Here I have only tried to sketch the broad contours of recent developments. Most of the story I have recounted has been about the life on the land before resettlement. I observed life in the settlement only during its initial phase, and for the most part have limited my narrative to that. My hope is that a young Inuk anthropologist will become the ethnographer of the Tununermiut. What I have described is what I was witness to myself; beyond that I cannot go.

The Tununermiut have had to alter their life-styles many times since the *Kadluna* first entered their lands. My conviction is that they have forged their own responses and created their own adaptations to all of these impositions from the outside, including the drastic ones that accompanied centralization. A way of life based on living on the land seemed temporarily to die, and like the older Tununermiut themselves, I grieved for its passing. Perhaps I was too hasty, for then, in the figurative flame of ethnic revitalization, it came alive once more, as a periodic alternative to hamlet living and a way of retaining ties with the past. Nevertheless, the new life is indeed based in the hamlet, and that hamlet is a part of a larger society and a shrinking world. Those facts cannot be changed.

It is my personal hope, as well as my prediction, that the Tununermiut will continue to take matters into their own hands, and in the process survive as a viable and distinct people within an industrial society.

WORKS CITED

The literature on the Inuit is vast. More has been published about them than possibly any other human society which has fallen under anthropological scrutiny. There are also the accounts of travelers, missionaries, and others. Perhaps it is not trite to say, in reference to the Inuit, that to meet them is to write about them.

This work is a study of what happened among one small Inuit population on northern Baffin Island in a relatively short period of time. Were it more comprehensive, a full bibliography would be included. The following is simply a list of works referred to in this book, and does not pretend to be even an abbreviated listing of sources concerning the Inuit.

Bernier, Joseph. 1909. *Report on the Dominion Government expedition to the Arctic Islands and the Hudson Strait on board the C.G.S. "Arctic." 1906–7* Ottawa: Canadian Department of Marine and Fisheries.

Berreman, Gerald D. 1962. *Behind many masks: Society for Applied Anthropology*. Ithaca, NY.

Briggs, Jean. 1974. "Eskimo women: Makers of men." In Matthiasson, Carolyn, ed. *Many Sisters: Women in Cross-Cultural Perspective*. New York: The Free Press 261-304.

Chance, Norman A. 1960. "Culture, change and integration: An Eskimo example." *American Anthropologist* 66:1028-44.

Flanagan, R.T. 1963. *A history of the Department of Northern Affairs and National Resources in its various manifestations since 1867 with special reference to its role in the existing Northwest Territories*. Unpublished manuscript. Ottawa: Department of Northern Affairs and National Resources Library.

Graburn, Nelson. 1969. *Eskimos without igloos: Social and economic development in Sugluk*. Boston: Little, Brown.

Helm, June, and David Damas. 1963. "The contact-traditional all-native community of the Canadian north." *Anthropologica*, n.s. 5:9-21.

Honigmann, John J., and Irma Honigmann. 1965. *Eskimo townsmen*. Ottawa: Canadian Research Centre for Anthropology.

Janes, Robert. n.d. *Diary*. Ottawa: National Archives of Canada.

Jenness, Diamond. 1936. The village of the crossroads. *Forest and Outdoors* 32:14-20.

Lesage, Jean. 1955. Enter the European. *The Beaver* (Spring) 285:3-9.

Low, A.P. 1906. *Cruise of the Neptune: Report of the Dominion Government expedition to Hudson Bay and the Arctic Islands on board the D.G.S.* Neptune *1903-4*. Ottawa: Government Printing House.

Marie-Rousseliere, Guy. 1957. Longevity among the Eskimo. *Eskimo* 43:13-15.

Matthiasson, John S. 1974. You scratch my back and I'll scratch yours: Continuities in Inuit social relations. *Arctic Anthropology* 12:31-36.

McConnell, John. 1976. The dialectic nature of Eskimo culture. In *Consequences of economic change in circumpolar regions*, ed. L. Muller-Wille, Edmonton: Institute for Northern Studies 201-13.

Morice, Adrian G. 1943. *Thawing out the Eskimo*. Trans. Mary T. Loughlin, Boston: Society for the Propagation of the Faith.

Mutch, James S. 1906. Whaling in Ponds Bay. In *Boas Anniversary Volume. Anthropological Papers Written in Honor of Franz Boas*. New York: G.E. Stechart. (pagination not available)

Ordinances of the Northwest Territories. 1963. Ottawa: Queen's Printer.

Report of the Royal Canadian Mounted Police for the year ended September 30, 1921. 1922. Ottawa: King's Printer.

Report of the Royal Canadian Mounted Police for the year ended September 30, 1923. 1924. Ottawa: King's Printer.

Robertson, Douglas S. 1934. *To the Arctic with the Mounties*. Toronto: Macmillan.

Service Contract of the Toonoonik-Sahoonik Co-operative Ltd. for 1973–74. 1973. Pond Inlet, NWT.

Steele, Harwood. n.d. *Policing the Arctic: the Story of the Conquest of the Arctic by the Royal Canadian (formerly North-West) Mounted Police*, Toronto: Ryerson.

Vallee, Frank. 1962. *Kabloona and Eskimo in the Central Keewatin*. Ottawa: Northern Coordination and Research Centre.

Van Norman. 1951. Life at an eastern Arctic detachment. *Royal Canadian Mounted Police Quarterly*. 17 (pagination not available)

Wilkinson, Doug. 1955. *Land of the long day*. Toronto: Clarke, Irwin.

Printed in Canada